AF669202

THE TALUQDARI SETTLEMENT IN OUDH

The Taluqdari Settlement in Oudh

RAJKUMAR SARVADHIKARI

" Quoth Hudibras, 'I smell a rat';
Ralpho, thou dost prevaricate."

" Truth crushed to earth shall rise again:
The eternal years of God are hers;
But Error, woulded, writhes with pain,
And dies among his worshippers."

MANOHAR
2020

First published 1882
Reprinted 1985, 2020

© Manohar Publishers & Distributors

All rights reserved. No part of this publication may be reproduced or transmitted, in any form or by any means, without prior permission of the publisher.

ISBN 978-81-944962-3-6

Published by
Ajay Kumar Jain *for*
Manohar Publishers & Distributors
4753/23 Ansari Road, Daryaganj
New Delhi 110 002

Printed at
Replika Press Pvt. Ltd.

PREFACE.

I HAVE endeavoured in the following pages to write a succinct history of the Taluqdari Settlement in Oudh. My principal object has been to narrate the history in the very words of the great Statesmen and Administrators who have been the authors of the settlement. My materials have been principally derived from Parliamentary Blue Books, Official Reports and Returns, and other State Papers. I have not hesitated to use the exact language of the documents, in my earnest wish to give a clear and authoritative exposition of the fundamental principles upon which the Taluqdari system is based. I have tried to present an impartial view of the great issue between the landlords and tenants in this Province. The passionate advocates of tenant - rights have, in their philanthropic desire to ameliorate the condition of the Oudh peasantry, scouted the idea of *ancient hereditary* rights in Oudh, and failed to evince due respect for the permanent proprietary rights guaranteed by the British Government. It is a mistake in principle, even as a political measure, to rob—in the language of a familiar proverb—Peter to pay Paul. The relations between landlords and tenants in this Province have been entirely misconceived. The Taluqdari system has been declared by high authority to be "the ancient, indigenous, and cherished system of the country." "The feudal attachments of landlord and tenant," as Sir George Couper justly remarked, "are not yet dead in the ancient baronies of Oudh." They are not only "not dead," but it can be unmistakably proved that the true spirit—the *ethos*—of feudalism is still in its pristine vigour in many parts of the *Garden of India.* Any attempt to destroy the authority of the taluqdars in their estates, and to disturb the filial relations that exist between them and their tenants, is a thing to be deprecated and deplored by all true friends of Oudh. The proper course of action of every one who has the lasting welfare of the Province at heart, should be not to attempt to undermine proprietary rights and to set the tenants against their landlords, but to convince *misguided* landlords that their interests are closely bound up with those of their tenants, and that their true strength lies in the happiness and prosperity of those who hold under them. To try to decry the Taluqdari system with a view to raise the present status of the *ryots* of Oudh, is likely to result in nothing more than in engendering bitter feelings between the landlords and their tenants, and thus defeat the very object our philanthropists set before them. Their aim should be not to sneer at the patriarchal institutions of India and to rudely shake the existing feudal organization of the country, but to endeavour to combine *order* with *progress*—the statical with the dynamical forces of society. Progress is then alone placed on firm ground, when it is based on *order*.

CONTENTS.

CHAPTER IV.

CHAPTER V.

CHAPTER VI.

CHAPTER VII.

CHAPTER VIII.

THE

TALUQDARI SETTLEMENT IN OUDH.

I.—LORD CANNING'S OUDH PROCLAMATION.

THE *fiat* had gone forth. Lord Canning hurled his bull from Allahabad. The 15th of March 1858 was a memorable day for Oudh. The Governor-General in his wrath confiscated the land of Oudh, with the exception of the estates of six loyal chiefs. "The proprietary right in the soil of the province," said the Governor-General in a voice of thunder, "is confiscated to the British Government, which will dispose of that right in such manner as may seem fitting." It was announced to those land-holders, however, who would make an immediate unconditional surrender, that their lives would be spared, "provided their hands are unstained by English blood murderously shed;" but it was declared that, "as regards any further indulgence which may be extended to them, and the condition in which they may hereafter be placed, they must throw themselves upon the justice and mercy of the British Government."

This Proclamation caused real alarm in the country. Not one voice was raised in its defence. It was sincerely believed that the Proclamation was of such a character that the flames of war would never be quenched in Oudh. It was severely censured by Lord Ellenborough, the President of the Board of Control. "Other conquerors," indignantly wrote this nobleman to Lord

Canning, "when they have succeeded in overcoming resistance, have excepted a few persons as still deserving of punishment, but have with a generous policy extended their clemency to the great body of the people. You have acted upon a different principle; you have reserved a few as deserving of special favour, and you have struck with what they feel as the severest of punishment the mass of the inhabitants of the country. We cannot but think that the precedents from which you have departed appear to have been conceived in a spirit of wisdom superior to that which appears in the precedent you have made." Mr. Bright also, with his characteristic eloquence, denounced it in strong language in the House of Commons: "What is the meaning," indignantly asked the eloquent Member for Birmingham, "of confiscating the proprietary rights in the soil? We have heard from a Noble Lord in 'another place,' and it has been stated in the course of the debate here, that this sentence of confiscation refers only to certain unpleasing persons who are called Taluqdars, who are barons and robber chiefs and oppressors of the people (!!)" This is by no means the first time that, after a great wrong has been committed, the wrong-doer has attempted to injure by calumny those upon whom the wrong has been inflicted.

"The history of our connection with the country," he continued, "whose interests we are now discussing, is of a nature that ought to make us pause before we consent to any measure that shall fill up the cup of injury which we have offered to the lips of that people. Two years ago we deposed the sovereign of Oudh. Everything that he had was seized; much of it was sold. Indignities were offered to his family. Their ruin was accomplished, though they were the governors of that kingdom. Some honourable Gentlemen, speaking on this side of the House, have tried to persuade the House that this confiscation-policy only intends that we should receive the taxes of Oudh. But that is altogether a delusion. That is a statement so absurd that I am astonished that any one should offer it to the House. In 1856, when you dethroned the king of Oudh, you stepped into his place, and became the recipients of all the legitimate national taxes of the kingdom of Oudh; and now, having seized the 500,000*l* a year, the revenue of that country, after a solemn treaty which contained a clause that if there were a surplus of revenue it should be paid to the credit of the kingdom of Oudh,—after having applied that surplus, contrary to the clause of that treaty, to the general purposes of India, you now step in and you descend below the king, to every taluqdar—to every landowner, large or small—to every man who has proprietary rights in the soil—to every man the smallest and humblest capitalist who cultivates the soil. To every one of these you say, in language that cannot be mistaken, come down from the independence and dignity you have held. As we have done in other provinces in India we shall do here. Two-thirds of you have not been mixed up in this war; but in this general confiscation the innocent must suffer with the guilty, for such is the misfortune of war, and such is the penalty which we shall inflict upon you." In this way even the great radical reformer condemned the dead-level system, which it was supposed at the time the India Government contemplated introducing into Oudh. The feeling was almost universal that the proprietary rights of the large taluqdars and landowners were overturned without just cause. Some of the newspapers in India upheld this confiscation-policy, "because they said that at one fell swoop it had done that which it took us twenty years to do in other districts of India." The great advocate of the rights of the people condemned in such strong language the confiscation-policy of Lord Canning, because he believed that a cruel wrong was done to the landowners of Oudh, and that, by sweeping away all proprietary rights in the soil, the rich proprietors of the Garden of India "would be reduced to mere tillers of the soil, whose share of the produce of the land they would cultivate would only be a handful of rice per day!"

In the Province of Oudh the princes and the peasants were equally terrified. There was but one course left — to burn the women and the children on a huge funeral pyre and die, like the Hindu heroes of old, sword in hand. The feeling of consternation caused by the Proclamation was so intense, that even those who were ready to make an unconditional surrender wavered in their resolution, and would not venture out from their strong fortresses to make their submission.

The Governor-General said, it is true, "that he would be ready to view liberally the claims, which those who would promptly come forward to aid in the restoration of order might acquire to a restitution of their former rights." But these words were unmeaning to most of them. No flag of truce was unfurled, and the destroying angel met the people face to face. They cowered through fear, and in some cases desperation inspired them with courage. Beni Madho was not the only landowner who, believing that his case was desperate, fought to the last, and was at length obliged to fly from the province and die an ignominous death. Beni Madho's fate would have been that of many others if the British Government had not extended to the province the hand of mercy and forgiveness. Had Lord Canning delayed to proclaim a large, generous, and general amnesty to the people of Oudh, this fine province would soon have been, to use an oriental metaphor, the favourite abode of pallid ghosts and screeching owls.

There were many people in India at that time who did not understand the real motives of Lord Canning in issuing this Proclamation. The policy was pronounced to be, without a single dissentient voice, too harsh and despotic. Even Sir James Outram, who, it was well known, had the support and confidence of the Governor-General in the discharge of his high duties, put a wrong interpretation upon it. He pointed out to Lord Canning that the effects of the confiscation-policy would be most disastrous to the province. It would make all the landholders desperate, and the result would be "a guerilla war for the extirpation, root and branch, of this class of men, which will involve the loss of thousands of Europeans by battle, disease, and exposure." Nothing, however, could have been further from the thoughts of "Clemency Canning" than a wholesale confiscation of the proprietary rights in Oudh. Pressure of work prevented him from giving full explanations to the Home Government regarding the real scope and object of the Proclamation. He wrote, however, a private letter to Mr.

Vernon Smith, the predecessor of Lord Ellenborough, who, Lord Canning believed, was still at the head of the Board of Control, to the effect that the Proclamation would be unintelligible without further explanations, and that these explanations would follow. He addressed a letter also to Lord Granville to the same effect. Had his explanations reached England before the memorable debate in the House of Commons took place, Lord Canning would have been spared much unmerited invective. His real object in issuing the Proclamation was entirely different from what it was represented to be at that time.

"It is just possible," said Mr. Bright, "that Lord Canning is in the midst of circumstances which have rendered it very difficult, perhaps impossible, for him to exercise his own calm judgment on the great question which forms the subject of this Proclamation. I see in that Proclamation not so much an emanation from the humane and just mind of Lord Canning as the offspring of that mixture of red tape and ancient tradition, which is the foundation of the policy of the old Civilian Council of Calcutta." Mr. Bright did not know at the time that this Proclamation was emphatically a product of his Lordship's "own calm judgment,"—a faultless "emanation" from the humane and just mind of Lord Canning,—a visible token of his mercy and clemency towards those great chiefs upon whom a cruel wrong had been inflicted by the mistaken revenue policy of Lord Dalhousie. We have it upon credible authority that Lord Canning showed the original draft of the Proclamation in his own handwriting to Sir George Campbell, the late Lieutenant-Governor of Bengal, who was then in immediate communication with his Lordship. Lord Canning told Sir George himself, before the Proclamation was published, "that his object was not really to confiscate finally the rights of the taluqdars, but to get rid of all the engagements into which we had entered after Annexation, and to obtain a *tabula rasa*, which would enable him to restore the great landowners, and to redress the injustice which he thought they had suffered, on condition of their full and complete allegiance." "In fact," says Sir George Campbell, "the step was taken in pursuance of a policy the opposite of that which had before prevailed, and in order to clear the ground for the new system." The real intention of the Proclamation was thus broadly and generally explained in the Governor-General's despatch of the 17th of June to the Secret Committee: "I apprehended little difficulty," said Lord Canning, "and so far as experience has gone, little has, I believe, been found in explaining to the taluqdars and landowners with whom our officers have come in contact, that the confiscation does not necessarily operate as a permanent deprivation of their rights, but that it places in the hands of Government the power of punishing those who shall persist in rebellion after life and honor have been guaranteed to them,—of rewarding those who shall promptly come forward and give their support to the Government and to the cause of order,—of substituting, in every case of restoration, the undeniable title derived from the will of Government for the doubtful title which alone could be advanced by the majority of those whom the order affected,—and of attaching to the fiat of restoration such conditions of service (political and military), fealty and good conduct as the altered circumstances of the province have made essential to the firm establishment of our authority." The principle of his policy, in the language of an eloquent writer, was somewhat like that adopted by Lord Durham in Canada. It put aside the technical authority of law for the moment, in order that a reign of genuine law might be inaugurated. It seized the power of a dictator over life and property, that the dictator might be able to restore peace and order at the least cost in loss and suffering to the province and the population whose affairs it was his task to administer.

In January 1858, long before the Proclamation of March was issued, Sir James Outram had thus written to the Governor-General regarding the system of civil administration which should be introduced into the province after the subjugation of Lucknow:

"A reasonable time, say one month, should be allowed to the people to come into the head-quarters of the nearest Civil Authority, and lay down their arms, for which a liberal price should be given. But that time once expired, the penalty for possessing arms should be death, and the stern decree should be rigidly enforced. Only a few examples will be required, and the disarming will then be effectual, as concealed weapons will be at once melted down, or otherwise destroyed. But I am convinced that nothing short of this measure will effect it, and that, unless the law be rigidly carried out, we shall never be able to restore perfect tranquillity to this portion of our dominions. The active co-operation of the landholders must be obtained, and this can best be done by declaring that the Government will regard the life of the offender as a sufficient expiation of the first offence against the provisions of the Proclamation, committed on lands held by the same proprietor, or body of proprietors. But that if a second instance of the possession or concealment of arms on the same estate occur, the entire rights and interests of the owner of the land will be liable to confiscation. One such example will convince the lawless landholders of Oudh that the British Government is in earnest, and that they have at last met with their master.

"The system of settlement with the so-called village proprietors will not answer at present, if ever, in Oudh.

"These men have not influence and weight enough to aid us in restoring order. The lands of men who have taken an active part against us should be largely confiscated, in order, among other reasons, to enable us to reward others in the manner most acceptable to a native. But I see no prospect of restoring tranquillity except by having recourse, for the next few years, to the old taluqdari system.

"The taluqdars have both power and influence to exercise either for or against us. The village proprietors have neither.

"Taluquas should only be given to men who have actively aided us, or who, having been inactive men, evince a true willingness to serve us, and are possessed of influence sufficient to make their support of real value.

"There will be no difficulty in settling the rent to be paid from each taluqa, and this should be distributed ratably over the several constituent villages; the exact amount to be paid by each villager to be settled among themselves. By this arrangement the taluqdar will be unable to raise his rents, and he should, moreover, be given to understand that, on his treatment of the people under him, his admission to engage at the revised settlement would, in a great measure, depend.*

"This, in my opinion, would suffice for the protection of a body of men, not one of whom, not even those with whom the settlement was made to the exclusion of the old taluqdars (some of eighty years' possession!) have come forward to aid us in this juncture. The taluqdar should be responsible for the disarming of the population, the destruction of the forts, and the apprehension of offenders within the limits of his estate. He should be made to feel that he holds upon a strictly 'service' tenure, dependent entirely on the punctual discharge of his duties as a landholder. *Very* influential men, or men who have done real good service during the present crisis, might have a portion of land in *jagheer*, conditional on constant and zealous service. This measure would enlist this powerful body of men on our side, while it entails no injustice on the cultivators of the soil, who have been accustomed all their lives to the taluqdari tenure, with power on the part of the taluqdar to raise his rents *ad libitum*. In a word, the men capable of restoring order and confidence will be gained over, while the men who will be benefited by the restoration, but who will never move a hand or foot to obtain or hold such a blessing for themselves, will suffer no hardship and be in a much better condition than they were before Annexation."

This was Sir James Outram's idea of the taluqdari system, which he advised the Governor-General to introduce into Oudh immediately after the pacification of the province. His system was only a modified village system of the Thomasonian school. Be that as it may, it is abundantly clear from the extract given above that Sir James Outram was strongly convinced of the utter worthlessness of the revenue-arrangement made by Lord Dalhousie in Oudh at the annexation of the province.

* Sir James Outram's language would appear, at first sight, to be against the taluqdar being made absolute proprietor. He evidently does not mean anything more than that the rights of under-proprietors should be protected. Oudh legislation has now secured this result.

This was the officer who, as Resident at Luckow, recommended the annexation of Oudh. This was the officer who was selected by the great autocrat at Calcutta to give effect to the policy which by a foregone conclusion he had determined to adopt in Oudh. "That the duty to the performance of which he was summoned was distasteful to him is not to be doubted. His sympathies had always been with the native princes of India. He hastened to Oudh, and carried out Lord Dalhousie's orders with as much kindliness of manner as it was possible to throw into such rough work."*

Sir James Outram entirely disapproved of the policy announced in the Proclamation of March. He felt himself unable to carry out this policy. He was for a liberal treatment of all persons who were "misled, but who desired to return to the path of duty." Though he received permission from Lord Canning to offer more liberal terms than were contained in the Proclamation to the landholders, still he did not wish to retain his post, and he requested the Governor-General to be relieved of his duties. Mr. (afterwards Sir Robert) Montgomery was appointed Chief Commissioner in place of General Outram. The new Chief Commissioner is described as "a man of peculiar smoothness of manner and appearance, a large vigorous head, a clear good eye, and great firmness of mouth and lip." He was understood to have obtained permission from Lord Canning to modify the menaces of the Proclamation, and to offer considerable "concessions" to the landholders of the province. It was almost universally felt at the time that the taluqdars had been hardly dealt with, and that, therefore, they required greater consideration than the chiefs in other parts of India in those terrible times. Oudh was in a state of complete anarchy, and it required great tact and skill and considerable administrative ability to re-establish good government, peace, and order. Sir Robert had thus a grand task before him, and, as subsequent events showed, he was thoroughly suited to the work, and the glory of accomplishing it was as great as the labour.

* Dr. Russel.

II.—THE ROYAL PROCLAMATION.

On the first of November 1858, the Royal Proclamation containing solemn promises of mercy, pardon, and forgiveness, was read at Allahabad to a large assemblage of princes and chiefs by the first Viceroy of India. Marked allusion was made in it to the Province of Oudh and the Proclamation of March:

"Already in one province, with a view to stop the further effusion of blood, and hasten the pacification of our Indian dominions, our Viceroy and Governor-General has held out the expectation of pardon on certain terms to the great majority of those who, in the late unhappy disturbances, have been guilty of offences against our Government, and has declared the punishment which will be inflicted on those whose crimes place them beyond the reach of forgiveness. We approve and confirm the said act of our Viceroy and Governor-General, and do further announce and proclaim as follows:—

"Our clemency will be extended to all offenders, save and except those who have been and shall be convicted of having directly taken part in the murder of British subjects. With regard to such the demands of justice forbid the exercise of mercy.

"To those who have willingly given asylum to murderers, knowing them to be such, or who may have acted as leaders and instigators in revolt, their lives alone can be guaranteed; but in apportioning the penalty due to such persons, full consideration will be given to the circumstances under which they have been induced to throw off their allegiance, and large indulgence will be shown to those whose crimes may appear to have originated in a too credulous acceptance of the false reports circulated by designing men.

"To all others in arms against the Government we hereby promise unconditional pardon, amnesty, and oblivion of all offences against ourselves, our crown and dignity, on their return to their homes and peaceful pursuits.

"It is our royal pleasure that these terms of grace and amnesty should be extended to all those who comply with their conditions before the first day of January next."

III.—CONCILIATORY MEASURES.

The state of Oudh caused great anxiety to the Government. Lord Canning earnestly wished to restore tranquillity to this troubled province, which had so long been devastated by war. But neither the thunders of the Commander-in-Chief, — the terrible bulls fulminated by the Governor-General from Allahabad,—nor the threats and menaces of the Chief Commissioner produced any effect on the Chieftains of Oudh. General Barrow (then Major), whose coolness and gallantry in the field, and whose sympathies with native chiefs eminently fitted him for the task with which he was entrusted, was appointed Special Commissioner, with extraordinary powers, to offer liberal terms to the landholders in order to induce these powerful chiefs to become the friends and supporters of Government. For a long time the eloquent persuasions of this kind-hearted officer, whose memory is fondly cherished by every native of Oudh with tears of affection, made no impression upon the taluqdars. They still held back. Powerful nobles and influential native gentlemen were employed to exercise their influence on behalf of the British Government. Nothing would induce the taluqdars to believe that the intentions of the British Government were honorable. In vain were they told that the word of the British Sovereign once pledged was pledged for ever. In vain were they told that the solemn engagements into which the British Government entered would never he disturbed again. They pointed with sadness to the proceedings at the settlement immediately after Annexation, when the estates of all the taluqdars were in the first instance resettled with them, and *kabuliyats* were taken from them exactly similar to their existing engagements with the superseded Government. These engagements lasted but for one season, when the officers of the British Government turned a deaf ear to all their prayers and solicitations, settled their estates with tenants and dependents, and ejected them from their homes and fields without mercy. In vain were they told that the fair city of Lucknow had been rased to the ground, and destruction would inevitably follow their protracted contumacy. No heed whatever was given to these threats and menaces. In vain were they told that bygones would be bygones, that their property and reasonable claims would be respected, and that any injustice of which they could fairly complain would at once be redressed. These empty statements carried no weight with them. Lord Canning became impatient. Sir Robert Montgomery determined to overcome all difficulties. General Barrow was summoned to Allahabad. Lord Canning impressed upon him the absolute necessity of restoring peace and order in Oudh. The Chief Commissioner desired him to restore order "with all the means at his disposal."

General Barrow was instructed to make most unreserved promises, and most unreserved promises were made. "There was in Oudh at this time," says the Special Commissioner, "a 'peace-at-any-price' party, backed and urged on by the highest authorities." The difficulties of this gallant officer were enhanced by false and evil reports which were circulated at the time by designing men who were beyond the pale of mercy and pardon. The people were gravely told that all persons returning to Lucknow would be made Christians, and that those who would not present themselves would be hanged, and die a felon's death. Credulous as the people were, these groundless rumours were implicitly believed. But Sir Robert Montgomery and his worthy assistant, who thoroughly knew the good traits of native character, were not daunted by these difficulties. Proclamations of amnesty were issued, and circular-letters containing promises of pardon and forgiveness were addressed to all the taluqdars. They were invited to make their submission under a *promise* of having restored to them the estates they held at Annexation. "A pass," says General Barrow in his Notification of 23rd June 1858, "is attached permitting you to come unmolested to Lucknow. On arrival there the terms of the *kabuliyat* and *patta* will be explained to you; and if you do not wish to agree to them, you will be allowed to return. The time allowed in the pass is thirty days." It is quite clear from this, said Sir Charles Wingfield in 1866, in a minute addressed to the Governor-General, in reference to General Barrow's Notification quoted above, that the taluqdars, who were still in arms against the British Government, were regarded more in the light of belligerents than of rebels, and that they were invited to come to Lucknow under a safe conduct to hear the terms of peace, rather than the conditions of pardon.

Mr. Bright, in the speech from which I have already quoted, says:—"There are certain matters which I understand all sides of the House to be agreed on. They agree with the Government and the East India Company that the people of Oudh are enemies, but that they are not rebels. The East India Directors—and they are likely to know, for they were connected with the commission of the act that brought this disturbance in Oudh upon us—say that the people of Oudh are not rebels, that they are not to be treated as rebels, but as enemies. If so, the Government have a right to treat them according to those rules which are observed by nations which are at war with each other. Will the House accept that proposition? I am quite sure the people of England will accept that definition—that civilized Europe will accept it, and that history—history which will record our proceedings this night—will accept it."

By fair arguments and "politic treatment," the distrust of the taluqdars was removed. The main argument was the settlement as proprietor of his estate with each taluqdar as he presented himself. The taluqdars were not suddenly led on to yield their allegiance on account of a crushing defeat, but man by man they tendered their submission. As one came in another saw the treatment he received, and so gradually confidence was restored. "It was hardly a beaten foe," says the Special Commissioner, "who claimed mercy at our hands, but men yielding to a *politic invitation*, and relying, after their distrust was overcome, on the good faith of the British Government."

The stubborn resistance which the taluqdars hitherto maintained gave way, and in rapid succession they yielded. As soon as the Royal promises of general amnesty were made known, and solemn guarantees of an unreserved settlement were given, General Barrow was surrounded every day by powerful chiefs, who had newly returned to their allegiance. He is described by an eye-witness as having been "tossing about estates as large as shires and whole kingdoms with the wave of his hand, just as Napoleon used to fling away empires or a juggler knocks balls about. The scene was extremely interesting, and the particular coolness and self-possession of these men, who had been fighting against us a few hours before, and who now sat perfectly at their ease in the Special Commissioner's tent, were very striking. The present aspect of the country would indicate that the storm is over. Those who have escaped its fury are, with an anxious eye, scanning the clouds, fearful to trust themselves to believe in the calm, and for my part, I believe, it will be long indeed ere the roll and swell of the great waves shall have passed away."

This belief that it would be long before Oudh would be completely pacified, was unfounded. The prediction was falsified. On the 20th of December 1858, just one month and twenty days after the date of the Royal Proclamation, Lord Clyde informed the Governor-General that "the campaign was at an end, there being no longer even the vestige of rebellion in the Province of Oudh; and that the last remnant of the mutineers and insurgents had been hopelessly driven across the mountains, which form the barrier between the kingdom of Nepaul and Her Majesty's empire of Hindustan."

Sir Robert Montgomery was well aware of the extreme sensitiveness of native gentlemen regarding the treatment which they received from British officers. He was well aware of the contemptuous hauteur and supercilious scorn which were openly manifested towards native noblemen of the highest rank. They are not trained "to take chaff" good humouredly—to bear being laughed at. They have a nervousness about laughter—the feeling that it stings and is offensive; and in the presence of their superiors they have no "sense of the ludicrous." They expect punctilious courtesy alone from European gentlemen, and nothing more.

The Chief Commissioner was painfully aware of the *deficiencies* in this respect of the officers under him. Experience told him that one ungracious word in these critical times would mar all the good effects of the benevolent policy of Lord Canning. "Of what is a revolt composed?" asks Victor Hugo, and thus answers the question: "Of nothing and of every thing,—of an electricity suddenly disengaged,—of a flame which suddenly breaks out,—of a wandering strength and a passing breath." Now that the great landholders were returning to their allegiance, not without considerable fear lest their lengthened contumacy should be remembered against them in some way or other, it was very important that all officers entrusted with any share of the civil government should treat with due consideration the taluqdars and native gentry with whom they came in contact. A wide distinction was certainly to be drawn between those who had disgraced themselves by acts revolting to humanity, and those who, under a misguided policy, strove to assert their independence. "Honorable enemies," said the Chief Commissioner, "when vanquished, are still entitled to be treated with honor:" and he earnestly tried to impress on all officers that if it be desired to establish a firm and lasting government, that could not be done by the power of the sword alone, but by the courtesy and consideration with which the aristocracy of the country are treated, and are made to feel as lightly as possible the change of Government which tends to make all men equal. When men of rank and influence are required to attend on a District Officer, they should not be kept hanging about the Court, denied an audience, or communicated with through some native subordinate. Much of the unpopularity of the Courts in the province, after Annexation, was due to the fear which all native gentry entertain of the insolence and extortion of the subordinates, whose sordid interest it is to form themselves into a barrier between the Government and the people. All District Officers were directed not to summon native gentry unnecessarily, and to encourage them to come freely and discuss unreservedly with English officers affairs which interest them. Personal intercourse with the people was thus earnestly insisted upon by the Chief Commissioner, as upon it, more than on anything else, depended, in a great measure, the administrative success of District Officers in the province. Lord Canning also gave peremptory orders to strongly impress upon all the Civil Officers of the Government that any want of consideration, attention, and becoming courtesy to any class of the natives of the province, "whether they had been active rebels or not," would be viewed with the greatest displeasure, and would seriously impede the advancement of any officer who was guilty of it. These orders and exhortations are significant of the relations which existed at that time between the native gentlemen and officers of the Government. It is due to the officers of the Oudh Commission to say that these instructions to treat the taluqdars with courtesy and to be always accessible to them have been cordially attended to. The landholders have been always graciously received, and encouraged to talk of their own affairs and the difficulties they labour under. If they seek advice it is freely given to them, with that considerate suavity which makes it acceptable to the proudest noble. It is by this unrestrained and friendly intercourse between the officers of Government and the landed proprietors of Oudh, and by abstaining from unnecessary official interference with the latter, that the landed aristocracy and gentry of the province have become completely reconciled to the British rule, and have ceased to regret those absolute powers they exercised under the Native Government.

IV.—THE TALUQDARI SETTLEMENT.

The settlement operations did not commence till the end of November. A summary settlement, preparatory to a regular settlement, was determined upon. We find from a Memorandum which was submitted, in May 1858, by the Special Commissioner of Revenue, and approved by the Chief Commissioner, the lines of the policy which were then contemplated to guide the revenue arrangements after the pacification of the province. Reverting to the order of things in Oudh as regards possession of land at the time of Annexation, it was determined to *settle* with the taluqdars from whom engagements were taken by the Native Government, provided they became at once the adherents of the British rule. In settling with a taluqdar, a special engagement in general terms was to be taken from him not to deal harshly with his under-tenants, but care was to be taken not to interfere too particularly in his actual village collections. In respecting the rights of "old possession," no injury was intended to be done to the zemindars, who were to be protected from extortion. Experience showed that his natural position was under the old taluqdar, for it was found generally during the recent 'outbreak,' that he returned to his former subordinate post. If the zemindars, however, were found actually in *possession*, their rights were to be upheld. Rights in villages readjusted themselves in most cases during the late disturbances, and it was found not that the strong deposed the weak, but that the rightful lord regained possession of his own; and there were many instances in which the taluqdar did not repossess himself of his lost villages although he was in a position to do so. It was utterly impossible to attend to *minutiæ* at the summary settlement. The great object of the Government at this time was to restore peace and order to the country, and the easiest way to do this was to maintain the title of the party who was found in possession. This arrangement was expected to lead to the speedy pacification of the province. As all proprietary rights were forfeited by the confiscation order of March, and no person had any valid claim to any portion of the property he formerly possessed, Government had a legal title, apart from political reasons, to make its settlement with any person who would become a staunch supporter of the British rule, and materially aid the British authorities in re-establishing order in the province.

These were the lines of policy determined upon by the Oudh Government in May 1858; and on this basis settlement was made with those landowners who then tendered their allegiance. On the 6th of October, the Governor-General fully stated to the Chief Commissioner his views (which, he was aware, had already been "partially carried into effect in Oudh") regarding the system to be followed in the settlement of the land-revenue after the complete pacification of the province.

Recent events had very much shaken the Governor-General's faith in the stability of the village system even in the older provinces; and His Lordship was, therefore, all the more disposed to abandon it in a province to which it was unknown before the British rule was introduced in 1856. The Governor-General was well aware that, in some of the districts of the North-Western Provinces, the holders of villages belonging to taluqas which had been broken up at the settlement acknowledged the suzerainty of the taluqdar as soon as the British authority was subverted. They acted, in fact, as though they regarded the arrangement made at the settlement as valid, and to be maintained just so long as British rule lasted, and no longer, and as though they wished the taluqdar to reassert his former rights and reassume his ancient position over them at the first opportunity. Their conduct amounted almost to an admission that their own rights, whatever these might be, were subordinate to those of the taluqdar; that they did not value the recognition of those rights by the ruling authority; and that the taluqdari system was "the ancient indigenous and cherished system of the country." If such was the case in the older provinces, where the British system of government was established for more than half a century, during twenty years of which the British Government had done its best to uphold the interest of the village occupant against the interest and influence of the taluqdar, much more would the same feeling prevail in the Province of Oudh, where village occupancy, independent and free from subordination to the taluqdars, had been unknown. The Government endeavour "to better" (as it was thought at the time) the village occupants in Oudh was not appreciated by them. It may be true that these men had not influence and weight enough to aid the Government in restoring order, but they had *numbers;* and it can hardly be doubted, as the Governor-General justly remarked, that if they had valued their restored rights, they would have shown some signs of a willingness to support the Government which revived those rights; but they did nothing of the kind. The Governor-General was, therefore, of opinion that these village occupants as such deserved little consideration from the Government.

On these grounds, as well as because the taluqdars, if they would, could materially assist the Government in the re-establishment of the British authority and the restoration of tranquillity, the Governor-General determined that a taluqdari settlement should be made. His Lordship desired that it might be so framed as to secure the village occupants from extortion; that the tenures should be declared to be contingent on a certain specified service to be rendered; and that the assessment should be so moderate as to leave an ample margin for all expenses incidental to the performance of such service. The taluqdars might then be legitimately expected to aid the authorities by their personal influence and their own active co-operation, and they might be required to undertake all the duties and responsibilities which properly appertain to landholders; and these duties and responsibilities were to be rigidly exacted and enforced. With the declaration of these general principles, the Governor-General left the elaboration of the details to the judgment of the Chief Commissioner.

Even before the news of the complete pacification of the province reached the Home Government, the question of the settlement engaged the attention of Lord Stanley, Her Majesty's Secretary of State for India, almost at the same time as when Lord Canning issued his instructions to the Chief Commissioner of Oudh. Adverting to the revenue arrangements of 1856, His Lordship said, in his despatch to the Governor-General dated 13th October 1858, that the general tendency of the instructions issued by Lord Dalhousie's Government to the Chief Commissioner was to impress upon the officers of the Oudh Commission the expediency of making the settlement as much as possible in accordance with the system which had "brought the North-Western Provinces to a state of unexampled prosperity;" and the Commission were specially instructed "to improve and consolidate the popular institutions of the country by maintaining the village coparceneries and adapting our proceedings to the predilections of the people and the local laws to which they were accustomed." The Revenue Officers in Oudh, intent upon giving effect to these instructions, and laudably anxious to promote to the utmost the welfare of the great body of the agricultural classes, were not sufficiently regardful of the interests of the great landed proprietors, or aware of the dissatisfaction with which that class in the North-Western Provinces had been inspired by the settlement proceedings there; but did in many instances ignore their vested rights and overlooked them altogether in the three years' zemindari summary settlement, although unquestionably persons "actually in possession" at the time of the annexation of the country. This, said Lord Stanley, was undoubtedly an error. Many of these large landholders might have obtained possession of their holdings by means of violence and fraud.* But the British Government was not responsible for this; and as, by abstaining from summary interference with the existing state of things, no constructive promise was made to prolong it beyond the period of summary settlement, it would have been far better to tolerate for a time the possible injustice which you found in existence, than, by the introduction of sudden changes, to incur the risk of originating injustice of your own (to the great landholders). It was a natural tendency of the introduction of British rule in the province to embitter the feelings of this class of persons—the territorial aristocracy—against the British Government." But much of this bitterness might have been allayed by a more judicious and considerate course of procedure than that which was adopted in 1856; and the Secretary of State had no hesitation in recording his opinion that the Oudh Commission was injuriously precipitate where caution and deliberation were required; and where promptitude was demanded there was, in some cases, culpable delay.

The Secretary of State fully approved of the course of policy which was contemplated to be pursued towards the taluqdars of Oudh, which, it was hoped, would, by a fuller recognition of their ancient rights, secure their allegiance to the British Government. He exhorted the Governor-General to exercise a discriminating clemency or severity towards them, graduated in accordance with his knowledge of the part taken by them during the late disturbances; but, as a general rule, Lord Stanley prescribed oblivion of past offences as the only guarantee

* NOTE.—The expression "violence and fraud" here used is liable to produce a false impression. The majority of the taluqdars acquired their estates, not by "violence and fraud," but by purchase, gift, or inheritance. Their ancestors had in most cases been settled in Oudh for centuries. We are to understand the Secretary of State's language as implying that even if the taluqdars had acquired their estates by "violence and fraud," the British Government had no right to dispossess them, much less had the Government to do so, seeing that their title to possession was valid.

of the cordiality of future relations. The Governor-General was requested to endeavour, by wise and conciliatory personal explanations, to make the intentions of the British Government clearly understood, and not only by the restoration of their ancient rights, but also by liberal remission and advances to facilitate the agricultural operations, which must have been greatly obstructed by the recent disorganization of the country.

It is unquestionable, said Lord Canning in reply (25th November 1859), that the policy of Lord Dalhousie's Government at the time of Annexation was in accordance with that which had been pursued by Mr. Thomason with "great apparent" success. The instructions of Lord Dalhousie were plain and unequivocal, and left scarcely any choice to the local authorities, but to set aside the taluqdars, and to make the settlement with the parties *actually* in possession of the soil. The settlement was, of necessity, a summary one,—that is, it was less precise and detailed than a regular settlement would be, and it was avowedly to be revised after three years. Many, too, of the inferior officers employed in making it were of limited experience, because better trained officers could not be found. The orders of the Government were, in some instances, carried out with a want of discrimination which greater experience and sounder judgment might have corrected.

Lord Canning was fully convinced that the real feeling of the country unequivocally exhibited during the period of anarchy which followed the Mutinies disclosed or made more manifest defects in the land-revenue system of the North-Western Provinces, which could not safely be left out of mind when reorganizing the land tenures and administration of a new kingdom. The maintenance of a territorial aristocracy in India, wherever there was such an aristocracy still existing, was an object of so great importance that the Government wisely determined to sacrifice to it something of a system which, while it was believed to increase the independence and protect the *quasi*-rights of the cultivators of the soil, and perhaps slightly augment the revenue of the State, led more or less directly to the extinction or decay of the old nobility of the country.

How to preserve this class for useful purposes, and to prevent its impoverishment by idleness, extravagance, and dissipation, without recognizing exclusive rights and unequal laws in its favor, is a question which has always presented almost insuperable difficulties. But in Oudh, thought Lord Canning, there was a new and favorable opportunity of attempting the solution of the problem. The Government was, from the date of the confiscation order proclaimed in March 1858, free to take a new departure unencumbered by its previously declared adoption of a system similar to that of the North-Western Provinces. The system which has been chosen here is the old taluqdari system of the country, but modified and much guarded from abuse by the terms in which the new grants of their taluqas have been made to the taluqdars and their heirs, and accompanied by invitation and encouragement to some of the ablest amongst them to take part in the revenue administration and in the Magisterial duties of their districts.

The success which these measures have achieved has been fully proved by the administrative results of the last twenty-four years. It was by such measures as these alone that a permanent hold over the country could be obtained which should prove beneficial to all classes of its people. "We must work downwards," says the great statesman to whom Oudh owes a debt of eternal gratitude, "through the landed aristocracy and the old hereditary chiefs, carrying the best of them with us as regards their interests, and, if possible, as regards their feelings, but showing them that abuse of the authority which we entrust to them will be followed by discredit and loss to themselves. If we work upwards, elevating the village proprietors, while we thrust aside their heretofore arbitrary masters, not only curbing the power of the latter, but narrowing the field of their interests and occupations, we should succeed in nothing but in sowing dissension between the two classes of lords and cultivators of the soil, making discontented subjects of the first, and getting little gratitude from the second."

The wisdom of these remarks has been shown by the happiness and contentment of the people, and the rapid progress of Oudh under the system introduced into the province by Lord Canning's Government. The general confidence of all classes in the benevolent designs of the British Government has been firmly established, and the loyalty of its chiefs and people has been assured by the system which has restored harmony between them, and removed the cause of dissension which was sown between them by the mistaken policy of a benevolent Government. The taluqdars and other landholders have given ample evidence of being satisfied with the settlement that has been made with them, and of appreciating the liberal and considerate treatment they have received. The interests of the different classes of the community have been guarded and protected with jealous care, and the British character for justice and good faith has been vindicated with the utmost scrupulousness. It is impossible to overrate the importance of the salutary consequences of those beneficial measures of Lord Canning, by which the present system of Government has been adapted more to the character and the requirements of the people than that which was instituted on the first acquisition of the province. The taluqdars have fully justified the confidence which was reposed in them, and the signs of progress visible in all directions unquestionably demonstrate the success of Lord Canning's wise and benevolent policy. The improvement has been steady and progressive; the authority of the law is respected in all parts of the province ; the people have betaken themselves cheerfully to their industrial pursuits ; and a state of greater prosperity in Oudh than it has ever enjoyed can be confidently anticipated.

V.—THE SUMMARY SETTLEMENT.

General (then Major) Barrow proceeded steadily with the settlement operations. The summary settlement which was determined upon was fixed for three years' certain from 1st May, 1858, or until a detailed settlement could be carried out; but in the Gonda and Baraitch Districts, in which cultivation was very backward, it was extended to 1st May 1867.

The instructions conveyed in his Circular (January 28, 1859) by the Special Commissioner to the Revenue Officers leave no room for doubt as to the intention of the Government regarding the disposal of the rights in land under the settlement then in progress. By the terms of the Proclamation of March 1858, said General Barrow, the rights of the landholders, save a few specially exempted, were declared to be confiscated, and by this act all claims to estates at once ceased to be valid. Nevertheless, the Government, with due consideration for the interest of the people, restored their ancient rights to them subject to certain specified conditions. The primary condition of all land-tenures in Oudh was the recognition of the superior right of the taluqdars. In making the settlement then in progress, every individual case was carefully examined and rigidly scrutinized. The rights which were conferred on each holder of land were the free and incontestable grant from the paramount power, and could not be called in question. It was ordinarily the custom in making a summary settlement of revenue to enter into engagements with actual occupants, leaving the question of disputed right to be settled at some future settlement. Such a course was declared to be entirely wrong. The rights and claims of all parties were duly weighed; their conduct during the late disturbances, and their relations as regards taluqdars, were fully considered; and the decision in each case, which received the confirmation of the Chief Commissioner's approval, was to be considered *final and lasting.* There was no greater evil, said the Special Commissioner,—resulting as it did in the unsettling of men's minds, and in causing general uneasiness,—than that of referring claimants to some future tribunal where the whole question of rights in the soil might be argued and decided on some different principle. Whether right or wrong, certain principles had been laid down by the Supreme Government, and they were to be acted upon, and landholders were to be encouraged to feel that what they received then they would retain *for ever.* All Revenue Officers were desired to be guided by these instructions; were exhorted to endeavour to impress their tenor on all landholders within their jurisdiction; and were specially enjoined to refrain from referring disappointed claimants to any future settlement, because such a procedure would merely excite hopes which were sure to be frustrated.

It will be seen that this Circular clearly pointed out that the decisions with regard to proprietary claims, passed during the summary settlement and approved by the Chief Commissioner, must be considered *final.** Litigants were not to be referred to any future tribunal or future settlements; but landholders were to be encouraged to feel that what they received then they would retain *for ever.*

Mr. (afterwards Sir Charles) Wingfield, who had succeeded Sir Robert Montgomery as Chief Commissioner, earnestly represented to the Governor-General (June 4, 1859) that the information which he had acquired from persons most capable of judging, and from all parts of the province, convinced him that no class of the population believed in the long continuance of possession conferred by the summary settlement. The taluqdars, unable to realize such a departure† from the former system, thought that their estates were restored to them merely to purchase their submission and the speedy restoration to order; and they feared that they would be thrown over at the next settlement, as at Annexation, when they were admitted to engage for the revenue of a single harvest only. The village proprietors, on the other hand, with whom the *first* summary settlement was made after the Annexation, persuaded themselves that the British Government was only temporizing with the taluqdars and that when they would be rendered powerless by the destruction of their forts and surrender of their last gun, the taluqdars would be ejected in favor of the village proprietors, certainly at next settlement, if not sooner. A spirit of antagonism was thus kept alive. The taluqdars dreaded making any concession that might be construed hereafter into a recognition of this independent right of the village proprietors, and they would accept no benefit that might look like a renunciation of their own claims.

The remedy for this unsettled state of public feeling, in Sir Charles Wingfield's opinion, was easy. It consisted in the formal

---

* NOTE.—The settlement was *summary* so far as the fixing of revenue was concerned; but as regards proprietary right it was declared to be *final.*

† NOTE.—In the settlement which was made immediately after the Annexation, the policy was, as I have pointed out, to make a direct settlement with the occupants of the soil. Lord Canning's taluqdari policy was thus entirely different from that of Lord Dalhousie.

sanction of the Governor-General being given to the principle of the finality and perpetuity of the summary settlement then in progress, in respect to the proprietary right in the soil (as declared by Sir Robert Montgomery in Special Commissioner's Circular, dated 28th January 1859). Sir Charles Wingfield felt confident that if he could convey in every sunud given to a taluqdar an explicit assurance from the Governor-General to the above effect, conviction would force itself on all minds, and apprehensions and illusions would vanish. Any less unqualified assurance that the Chief Commissioner could give would be ineffectual. To say that the settlement was final, subject to the approval of the Governor-General, would rather tend to increase distrust. Sir Charles Wingfield, therefore, abstained from giving sunuds till he could do so in the manner pointed out by him. If an unreserved assurance of security could be given, the Chief Commissioner felt no doubt of the complete success of the taluqdari settlement.

The Chief Commissioner adopted stringent measures to secure for the village occupants immunity from extortion, as directed by the Governor-General in October 1858; but to establish the foundation of lasting contentment and prosperity, there must not be afforded the least ground for any expectation of change.

Sir Robert Montgomery, in his Circular dated 21st January, says Sir Charles Wingfield (July 15, 1859), declared the *finality* of *all* settlements, and though the present Chief Commissioner would prefer to see that order carried out in its integrity, he yet admitted that there were two very different classes of cases affected by it, and that while he considered it indispensable for the one, the other might, in his judgment, be without any inconvenience excluded from its operation.

The first class consisted of parties claiming separate interests in land, *viz.*, taluqdars and village proprietors—the superior and inferior parties. The Chief Commissioner strongly urged upon the Governor-General to declare *final* the settlement then made with the superior parties, in pursuance of the policy advisedly adopted by Government in consequence of the egregious failure of the opposite policy in 1856. He observed that, unless it was intended to depart from the present policy, and to do the very thing that the taluqdars dreaded,—namely, to exclude them at the next settlement and engage with the village proprietors,—there could be no objection to giving such an assurance as he proposed; and this was the view which the taluqdars also took of the matter. But if, as the Chief Commissioner firmly believed, no such departure was intended, he could not see the use of giving the village proprietors hopes of a rehearing at next settlement.

It must not be imagined that, in taluqdari estates, there had been conflicting claims of equal interests. Rarely did a taluqdar contend with another taluqdar for the title to land, and if ever such a dispute did arise, it was immediately disposed of by maintaining the *status quo* as it existed at the Annexation. The law of primogeniture, too, prevailed in the chief Hindu families, so there could be no disputes among the members.

It should also be well understood that no acquisitions made by taluqdars during the period of the recent disorganization of the province were confirmed at this settlement. The Government never gave a taluqdar, except in reward, a village that was not in his taluqa at Annexation; any change, therefore, that might be made at the next settlement could only be in favor of the village proprietors. The Chief Commissioner felt convinced that it was not intended to make any such change, but the taluqdars were not, and he wanted to assure them.

In short, said the Chief Commissioner, any objection there might be to declaring the settlement just made with men like Rajas Hunwunt Sing and Maun Sing, the Rajas of Amethee and Bulrampore, and a hundred others, perpetual in all but the assessment, must apply with equal force to the perpetual settlement of the Boondee Illaqa that had been made with the Raja of Kuppurthulla, for there were village proprietors in that estate as well.

The second class of cases was composed of parties claiming equal interests in the land, *viz.*, zemindar against zemindar. The estates that formed the subject of these disputes were generally small, and of zemindari, not taluqdari tenure; the claims generally turned on a question of inheritance from the last undoubted proprietor; and possession by either party was most difficult to prove, for the property had often changed hands (twenty times in as many years), the Native Government having dealt sometimes with one and sometimes with the other, and at intervals kept it under its own management, or leased it to a stranger.

There must be a limit, urged the Chief Commissioner, to the hearing of such claims. He very much doubted whether, by opening out such cases to renewed litigation, much substantial injustice would be remedied; still the measure involved no great principle. It would not shake the security of the settlement made with the taluqdar as against the village proprietors; the Chief Commissioner, therefore, did not oppose it. He simply confined his efforts to obtaining a guarantee against change at any time in the first class of cases, a point on which, he justly thought, the future of this province mainly hinged.

VI.—RESULTS OF THE SUMMARY SETTLEMENT.

General Barrow concluded the summary settlement in June, and submitted his report to the Chief Commissioner. The Special Commissioner explained that, immediately after the issue of the Proclamation of March 1858, when it had been determined to make the *status at annexation* the basis of the present summary settlement and to uphold the taluqdari system *as it then stood,* the landholders were called upon to tender their allegiance and receive back their estates. The consequence of this was that estates paying 52½ lakhs of rupees revenue were settled before the promulgation of Her Majesty's amnesty. The main object and principle of the settlement was to reconfer proprietary rights on persons possessing the strongest prescriptive title, and to impose a moderate assessment. The entire land-revenue assessed on the province under the settlement was 104 lakhs of rupees. Out of this amount, 77 lakhs were settled as they were before Annexation, and 14½ lakhs with the persons recognized in the settlement of 1856. These latter were chiefly proprietors of zemindari villages, which were in wrongful possession of contractors under the king's rule, and were restored in 1856 to their rightful owners. The remaining 12½ lakhs were from confiscated lands. Under the old settlement the taluqdars engaged for only 35 lakhs of the entire revenue; they were now admitted to engage for nearly 62 lakhs.

The Special Commissioner remarked that the taluqdars did not feel secure of being established in possession of their estates. They feared that as they were ousted from their estates after one season's settlement in 1856, so they should again be thrown over at the expiration of the present settlement. The under-proprietors who again submitted themselves during the late disturbances without a struggle to their feudal chief, recognizing his superior right, and giving him armed assistance to the last against the British authority, came forward (though not in large numbers) once more, after the pacification of the country, to claim their independence, and now vigilantly watched the slightest signs of the Government again relenting in their favor to resume their contest for proprietary rights. But amidst all this strife for rights it was remarkable how the taluqdars refrained from disputing each other's rights, and there were but rare instances on record of one seizing the other's estate. Even when a taluqdar had seized villages, during the period of disorganization, which he did not possess before, he rarely, if ever, preferred a claim to them at the present settlement. The Special Commissioner strongly recommended that a fair chance should be given to the present settlement; that adverse claims should be set at rest once for all; that the superior right of the taluqdar should be unflichingly supported; that the rights now conferred should be *firmly and fixedly* upheld; and that thus the formal sanction of the Government should be given to the principle of the finality and perpetuity of the summary settlement in respect to the proprietary right in the soil.

The Chief Commissioner was informed by telegram (October 6, 1859) that the Governor-General agreed generally with him in regard to the *absolute title* conferred on the taluqdars by the summary settlement.

The Governor-General, agreeing with the Chief Commissioner (October 10, 1859) as to the expediency of removing all doubts as to the intention of the Government to maintain the taluqdars in possesison of the taluqas for which they had been permitted to engage, was pleased to declare that every taluqdar with whom summary settlement had been made since the re-occupation of the province had thereby acquired a permanent hereditary and transferable proprietary right in the taluqa for which he had engaged, including the perpetual privilege of engaging with the Government for the revenue of the taluqa.

This right, however, was conceded, subject to any measure which the Government might think proper to take for the purpose of protecting the inferior zemindars and village occupants from extortion, and of upholding their rights in the soil in subordination to the taluqdars.

As regards zemindars and others not being taluqdars, added the Governor-General, with whom a summary settlement had been made, the orders conveyed in the limitation Circular of the 28th of January were not to be strictly observed. Opportunity was to be allowed at the next settlement to all disappointed claimants to bring forward their claims, and all such claims were to be heard and disposed of in the usual manner.

This declaratory order of the Government of India, of the 10th October 1859, which was implicitly sanctioned by the Secretary of State (April 24, 1860), is a rule or regulation which has the force of a Legislative Act (Indian Councils Act, sec. 25). It is, in form and substance, a declaratory enactment, intending to establish (and establishing in sufficiently clear terms) "the permanent, hereditary, and transferable proprietary right" of every taluqdar with whom the summary settlement was made.

The Chief Commissioner in reply expressed his strong conviction that anything less than an *unqualified* bestowal of the proprietary right on the taluqdars would not satisfy expectations or remove doubts. Of course there should be a condition in sunuds that they are bound to maintain all holding under them in all the rights they had heretofore enjoyed; the inferior zemindars would thus be effectually protected from wrong, and that was all that was wanted.

To embody in the sunuds the substance of the questionable *proviso* in the letter of the 10th October would, the Chief Commissioner was firmly persuaded, make matters worse than before. It would unsettle the minds of the inferior proprietors and encourage extravagant hopes of independence. It would alarm the taluqdars and make them regard the gift of the proprietary rights as a mockery and a delusion. It would, moreover, said Sir Charles Wingfield in a prophetic spirit, place an engine in the hands of any future Chief Commissioner and Governor-General adverse in principle to taluqdars, which would enable them to virtually annul the taluqdari settlement, and oust the taluqdars nearly as effectually as was done in 1856.

The only use that could be made of that *proviso* would be to enable the Government to make a sub-settlement between the taluqdar and the inferior proprietor, on the principle introduced by Mr. Thomason in the North-West. Such a sub-settlement would not practically differ from excluding the taluqdar altogether and engaging with the village proprietors as was done in 1856.

It is a bad principle to create two classes of recognized proprietors in one estate. Better do away with taluqdars altogether than confine them to a profit of eight or ten per cent., which is all that would be left them after deducting cost and risk of collection on the Government revenue for their incomes.

Of course this state of things would never come to pass so long as Lord Canning was at the head of the Government, but with a change in the Viceroyalty and in the Chief Commissionership, it would be brought about any day on the warrant of this proviso.

Sir Charles Wingfield was thus in a dilemma. If he inserted in the sunuds which were to be conferred on the taluqdars the substance of the proviso referred to, he would disgust the taluqdars and frustrate the object he laboured for; and if he suppressed it, and hereafter a sub-settlement was resolved upon, he afforded the taluqdars good ground for charging the Government with breach of faith.

If the object of Government, urged the Chief Commissioner, was not to make a sub-settlement at some future time, but merely to protect the village proprietors and uphold their rights, it would be adequately attained by the obligation it was proposed in the sunuds to impose on the taluqdars to maintain the inferior holders in the rights they enjoyed up to Annexation. Things were fast settling down, three-fourths of the *pattas* had been already given, and the taluqdars showed themselves disposed on all occasions to deal liberally and considerately with their tenants. The Chief Commissioner was fully convinced that the Government could do nothing so impolitic as to put new ideas and expectations into the minds of the latter.

VII.—SUNUD.

The form of the sunud, which was approved by the Governor-General, was as follows :—

" Know all men that whereas, by the Proclamation of March 1858 by His Excellency the Right Hon'ble the Viceroy and Governor-General of India, all proprietary rights in the soil of Oudh, with a few special exceptions, were confiscated and passed to the British Government, which became free to dispose of them as it pleased, I, ———, Chief Commissioner of Oudh, under the authority of His Excellency the Governor-General of India in Council, do hereby confer on you the full proprietary right, title, and possession of the estate of ———, consisting of the villages as per list attached to the *kabuliyat* you have executed, of which the present Government revenue in rupees is ———. Therefore this sunud is given you in order that it may be known to all whom it may concern, that the above estate has been conferred upon you and your heirs for ever, subject to the payment of such annual revenue as may from time to time be imposed, and to the conditions of surrendering all arms, destroying all forts, preventing and reporting crime, rendering any service you may be called upon to perform, and of showing constant good faith, loyalty, zeal, and attachment to the British Government, according to the provisions of the engagement which you have executed, the breach of any one of which at any time shall be held to annul the right and title now conferred on you and your heirs.

" But it is another condition of this grant, that, in the event of your dying intestate, or any of your successors dying intestate, the whole estate shall descend to the nearest male heir, such as sons, nephews, &c., according to the rule of primogeniture; but you and all your successors shall have full power to alienate the estate, either in whole or in part, by sale, mortgage, gift, bequest or adoption, to whomsoever you please.

"It is also a condition of this grant that you will, so far as is in your power, promote the agricultural prosperity of your estate, and that all holding under you shall be secured in the possession of all the subordinate rights they formerly enjoyed. As long as the obligations are observed by you and your heirs in good faith, so long will the British Government maintain you and your heirs as proprietors of the above-mentioned estate, in confirmation of which I herewith attach my seal and signature."

"The sunuds declare," wrote Lord Canning to the Chief Commissioner (October 19th, 1859), "that while, on the one hand, the Government had conferred on the taluqdars and their heirs *for ever* the full proprietary right in their respective estates, subject only to the payment of the annual revenue that might be imposed from time to time, and to certain conditions of loyalty and good service, on the other hand, all persons holding an interest in the land under the taluqdars will be secured in the possession of the subordinate rights which they have heretofore enjoyed.

"The meaning of this is, that when a regular settlement is made, wherever it is found that zemindars or other persons have held an interest in the soil intermediate between the ryot and the taluqdar, the amount or proportion payable by the intermediate holder to the taluqdar, and the net jumma finally payable by the taluqdar to the Government, will be fixed and recorded after careful and detailed survey and enquiry into each case, and will remain unchanged during the currency of the settlement, the taluqdar being, of course, free to improve his income and the value of his property by the reclamation of waste lands (unless in cases where usage has given the liberty of reclamation to the zemindar) and by other measures of which he will receive the full benefit at the end of the settlement. Where leases (*pattas*) are given to the subordinate zemindars, they will be given by the taluqdar, not by the Government.

"This being the position in which the taluqdars will be placed, they cannot with any show of reason complain if the Government takes effectual steps to re-establish and maintain in subordination to them the former rights, as they existed in 1855, of other persons whose connection with the soil is in many (?) cases more intimate and more ancient than theirs; and it is obvious that the only effectual protection which the Government can extend to these inferior holders is to define and record their rights and to limit the demand of the taluqdar as against such persons during the currency of the settlement to the amount fixed by Government as the basis of its own revenue demand."

The Governor-General agreed with the Chief Commissioner in his observation, that it was a bad principle to create two classes of recognized proprietors in one estate, and that it was likely to lead to the alienation of a larger proportion of the land-revenue than if there were only one class. But whilst the taluqdari tenure, notwithstanding this drawback, was about to be recognized and re-established, because it was consonant with the feelings and traditions of the whole people of Oudh, the zemindari tenure intermediate between the tenures of the taluqdar and the ryot was not a new creation, and it was a tenure which, in the opinion of the Governor-General, must be protected.

The Governor-General directed the Chief Commissioner to have ready by the end of October, when His Excellency expected to be at Lucknow, a list of the taluqdars on whom a permanent proprietary right was conferred. Lord Canning wished to bestow on these chiefs, with his own hand, the sunuds guaranteeing the permanent, hereditary, and transferable proprietary rights in the taluquas for which they had engaged.

VIII.—LORD CANNING'S FIRST DURBAR.

On the 26th October 1859, Lord Canning held his first Durbar at Lucknow for the reception of the taluqdars of Oudh and the chief native gentlemen of Lucknow, and for the distribution of rewards to all of every rank who rendered good service to the Government during the rebellion.

First, His Excellency gave a private audience to each of the nine principal taluqdars of the Province who protected and saved the lives of Europeans and other Christian subjects of the Queen at the commencement of the rebellion. These were the following :—

Maharaja Digbijaya Singh, of Bulrampore.
Maharaja Mansingh, of Shahgunj.
Raja Drigbijaya Singh, of Morarmow.
Raja Lal Madho Singh, of Gurh Amethee.
Raja Hanumant Singh, of Dharapore and Kalakankar.
Raja Hardeo Buksh, of Kaliaree.
Raja Rustum Shah, of Dera.
Baboo Ajit Singh, of Tiroul.
Raja Mardan Singh, of Burwara.

The whole of the taluqdars and other principal native gentlemen were then received by His Excellency in open Durbar, at which the Commander-in-Chief, the Chief Commissioner, and all the civil and military officers of the Government were present.

On the Viceroy taking his seat, the taluqdars were introduced to him one by one. They offered the usual nuzzurs, which were accepted.

Khilluts, titles, and other rewards in land and money were then conferred on those who, by good service during the rebellion, had deserved well of the British Government.

The Viceroy then addressed the assembly in the following words :—

"Taluqdars of Oudh,—I am glad to find myself in your country and amongst you, and to have this opportunity of speaking to you in the name of the Queen, your Sovereign.

"A year has now passed away since this Province was the seat of anarchy and war. The conduct of its people had been such that the Government was compelled to lay a heavy hand upon it. But peace and order are now restored to every corner of Oudh, and I am come to speak to you, not of the past, but of the future.

"You have all of you who are here present received yesterday the grants of those estates which the Government has restored to you. You will have seen by the terms of those grants that the ancient taluqdari system of Oudh is revived and perpetuated. Be assured, so long as each one of you is a loyal and faithful subject, and a just master, his rights and dignity as a taluqdar will be upheld by me, and by every representative of your Queen, and that no man shall disturb them. You will also have seen by those grants that the same rights are secured on the same conditions to your heirs for ever. Let this security be an encouragement to you to spend your care, and time, and money upon the improvement of your possessions. As the Government has been generous to you, so do you be generous to all those who hold under you down to the humblest tiller of the soil. Aid them by advances of money and by other indulgences to increase the productiveness of the land, and set them an example of order and obedience to your rules. Let the same security in your possessions encourage you to bring up yours sons in a manner befitting the position which they will hereafter occupy as the chiefs of Oudh. Learn yourselves, and teach them to look to the Government as a father.

"Taluqdars,—I trust there are none amongst you who are so infatuated as to believe that the Government has had designs against your religion. Even if there be any such, I will not condescend to repeat the assurances which they have already received on this head. I leave it to time and experience and their own sense to dispel their perverse suspicions. But for their own sakes, I warn them not to be led into acts of opposition or distrust towards the Government by the false tales of designing men.

"Lastly, Taluqdars, whenever in any matters you have doubts to be resolved or wishes to make known, address yourselves to the Chief Commissioner. He will tell you the truth in all things. He is the high and trusted representative of the Government in Oudh, and depend upon it, he will be your best adviser and your true friend.

"I wish that I could speak to you in your own language. That which I have said will be interpreted to you, and I enjoin you to bear it in your memories."

These words of Lord Canning, the great benefactor of Oudh,

are still ringing in the ears of the taluqdars. They are engraved in their memories, and will never be obliterated. These memorable words assured them, that *no man shall ever disturb* the permanent proprietary rights which were conferred on them, and that the same rights were *secured to their heirs for ever.*

IX.—CRITICISM OF THE SETTLEMENT BY SIR CHARLES WOOD.

The Secretary of State, in reviewing (April 24th, 1860) the administration of the province since its reoccupation, said, that he learned with satisfaction that the status in all taluqdari estates, as it existed at Annexation in 1856, had been virtually maintained. But he was rather doubtful as to the expediency of rendering, without giving the village proprietors sufficient time to prove their claims, the decisions of the Local Government regarding their alleged right *final and irrevocable.* If the claims of the taluqdars were just and right,—if, as was often urged, the feelings of the village proprietary bodies were in favor of the taluqdars, their interests would not have suffered by giving time to those who disputed them, while the Government would have had the satisfaction of knowing that substantial justice had been done. On the other hand, the delay would have given opportunity for the redress of any real wrongs which might have been inflicted. In what was thus set forth, it was by no means the object of Her Majesty's Government to advocate the revival of antiquated rights which had long passed out of the hands of the original owners; but that it would have been *politic* to have fixed a period within which all claims to the recovery of rights in the soil might have been heard. A period of twelve or even twenty years before the British rule, considering the state of misrule into which Oudh was plunged for some considerable period previous to Annexation, would have been fair and reasonable. The old influential families and the really ancient taluqdars, the heads of clans and races, would have lost little, perhaps nothing, by such a policy, while the native officials and followers of the

Court, who had risen to power by the lowest ways, would have had to disgorge some of their ill-gotten acquisitions.

The Secretary of State was fully sensible of the advantage of enlisting the loyalty and gratitude of the influential taluqdars on the side of the British Government, and trusted that they might be brought to regard the welfare of the State identical with their own, and that their zeal in the cause of order might be fostered by the measures which were adopted for associating them with the officers of the Government in the duties of maintaining the public peace, and conferring on them responsibilities which would still maintain their just pride in the prosperity of their estates.

The Secretary of State learned with satisfaction that such a wise policy of elevating, rather than of depressing, the local aristocracy was carried out by Lord Canning's Government. "Apprehensive," said the Secretary of State, "that the great taluqdars might regard with some suspicion a policy so obviously tending to produce the desired result of the general pacification of the country, you adopted measures calculated to give them confidence in the sincerity of your intentions and the stability of your arrangements. By personally addressing them in Durbar, and by causing sunuds to be issued confirming them, under certain conditions, in their proprietary rights, you have, I doubt not, effectually disarmed their suspicions and secured their loyalty, by identifying the fixity of their tenures with the stability of the Government under which they are held."

"The general progress of the province," wrote the Secretary of State to Lord Canning in 1861 (August 17), "appears to be of a most satisfactory character, and warrants me in offering my congratulations to your Excellency on the success which has attended the administrative efforts of your officers in a country so recently in a state of internal anarchy and convulsion.

"The system upon which you resolved to reconstruct the administration of Oudh, on the re-establishment of tranquillity in that province, was that of restoring to power and authority the taluqdars and other influential chiefs, whose rights and interests had not been sufficiently regarded in the arrangements made upon the first occupation of the country. To the principle of this measure Her Majesty's Government have already expressed their assent, and they have watched its operation with the liveliest interest. The liberal terms on which the taluqdars were restored to their old possessions, and on which grants of further lands were made, in reward for meritorious service, were well calculated to secure the zealous attachment of this class, and I rejoice to learn that they appreciate the benefits conferred upon them. Before the assumption of the administration of Oudh by the British Government, the more powerful landholders had lived in a perpetual state of antagonism to the sovereign authority and to the law of the land. But the experience of the past two years appears to justify the belief that this was the result of the system of Government under which they lived rather than of any inherent incapacity for better things. Under more kindly influences they have now begun to maintain the order they had violated, and to support the authority they had defied. And Her Majesty's Government are encouraged, by the reports now before them, to look with confidence to the progressive results of the policy which your Lordship has commenced, and which, I perceive with satisfaction, has been materially promoted by friendly intercourse between your officers and the principal landholders of the province."

X.—THE ABBOT CONTROVERSY.

In 1860, a controversy arose between the Chief Commissioner (Sir Charles Wingfield) and the Commissioner (Colonel Abbot) of the Lucknow Division with regard to the meaning of "taluqdar," and the effect of the Proclamation of March upon the subordinate rights in Oudh. Referring to this controversy, the Governor-General remarked (September 12, 1860), that it was the intention of the Government that all subordinate holders, unless specially deserving of punishment for persistent rebellion, should be restored to the rights they possessed before the rebellion, whether the parent estate were ancestral, acquired or conferred, and that every such holder should be maintained in his rights under the new guarantee precisely as if the taluqua had not been confiscated, or as if, having been confiscated, it had been settled with the hereditary taluqdar.

Generally, as regards the position of those who hold under the taluqdars, the intention of the Proclamation of 1858, and of every Act of Government that followed it, was a return to the condition of things which existed before the Annexation of Oudh and which had been altered in 1856 under the instructions issued on Annexation.

As regards the taluqdars, the intention of the Proclamation of 1858, and of the declarations made and measures taken in 1859 and subsequently, was: *first*, that, in replacing them in possession of their old estates, or in conferring upon them new estates (as the case might be), they should step into such possession, carrying with them the rights and authority which the taluqdars of those estates respectively held before Annexation, and which the action of the British officers in 1856 had impaired; and also carrying with them a new title derived from the Government, from whom alone, as their possession had been confiscated, any title could be derived: *secondly*, that the taluqdars should, by certain obligations imposed upon them, be restrained from the abuse of those rights and that authority.

The Governor-General assured the Chief Commissioner that he was quite right in saying that confiscation under the Proclamation of March 1858, where it had been carried out, annulled proprietary rights of every kind in the soil, inferior as well as superior, and in this sense confiscation was carried out throughout the province, except as regards the six estates specified in the Proclamation. It made no difference whether subsequently any particular estate was regranted to its former taluqdar, or was granted for the first time to a stranger. The Proclamation of confiscation had its effect in both cases, enabling the Government in both to revert to the order of things which existed before Annexation, and to superadd certain precautions against the abuses then practised.

It was a mistake to suppose that because an estate is now in the hands of the taluqdar, who held it under the British Government from the time of the Annexation to the time of the mutinies, the decree of confiscation has not taken effect on it. The effect of the Proclamation upon such an estate has been that it is now held under a direct title from the British Government, and that the relations which subsist between its taluqdar and the holders under him are those which subsisted between them before Annexation, modified or regulated by such obligations as the Government has imposed, not those which were established between them by the British officers acting under the instructions issued at Annexation.

CHAPTER II.

THIRTY YEARS' SETTLEMENT.

The Record of Rights.

ARRANGEMENTS were completed in 1860 for making a revenue settlement which would last for *thirty* years; and, in September of that year, the Chief Commissioner submitted to the Governor-General a copy of the instructions which he proposed to issue to officers entrusted with the regular settlement of Oudh. These instructions were all embodied in the famous "Record of Rights." The leading principle which it was intended to enforce was the maintenance of rights as they existed just before the Annexation, and no others. Sub-proprietors were to be secured in the possession of such rights as they were found in possession of in the Fusley year 1262-63, corresponding with 1854-55 *Anglice,* as in that year arrangements were entered into between the taluqdars and the intermediate holders which were known to have been favorable to the latter as regards the recognition of their rights. While maintaining the sub-proprietors in possession of the rights as above explained, it was not intended to depart from the fundamental principle of the land-revenue system of India, that the Government was entitled to a certain portion of the produce of the soil. The Supreme Government had determined that the broad principle that it is entitled to 50 per cent. of the gross rental was to be kept steadily in view; and where these sub-proprietors were found to have never paid to the taluqdar more than the Government demand, which might be fixed on an estimate of the gross rental, the taluqdar was to be permitted to take that much only *plus* 5 per cent. Where the intermediate holders, as sometimes happened, were found to have paid less than the Government demand fixed at settlement, they were to be compelled to pay the full demand *plus* 5 per cent. The

Supreme Government undertook to grant the taluqdars a fair compensation from the Government share, whenever it was found that the intermediate holders had intercepted a more than ordinary share of the aggregate profits of an entire taluqa.

The instructions contained in the Record of Rights appeared to the Governor-General (January 8, 1861) to be very just and proper, and to be framed in accordance with the views which the Government had already expressed.

As the 31st para. of the Record of Rights has led to much discussion and to adverse criticism, we will quote it in full.

It is as follows:—

"The Chief Commissioner has determined to make no distinction in the records between cultivators at fixed rates and cultivators-at-will. Abstractedly viewed, he considers that to give a title of permanent occupancy at an unvarying rent to the tiller of the soil, is an invasion of the rights of property, and a clog on enterprise and improvement. It must be shown that nothing less will suffice to guard the ryot from exaction, to justify such a measure. There is not the slightest possibility of this result happening in Oudh. Consequently, the measure is utterly unsuited to the province. In three-fourths of Oudh there is a deficiency of cultivators. These are so valuable that no landlord would seek to dispossess a good one; and a bad one he would be free to get rid of. Even in those parts where the population is more abundant, no symptom that the cultivator needs protection has been manifested. The question had not been stirred by the cultivators themselves. To create an element of present discord in order to provide against a contingency that cannot possibly occur for the next thirty years throughout these parts of the province, or for seven or eight years to come, at least in the remaining fourth, would demonstrate a wanton spirit of meddling. The abandoned and waste lands of Oudh will furnish occupation to any number of cultivators for many years to come; and if increase of population in the already thickly populated districts of the south-east of Oudh should eventually have the effect of driving cultivators across the Gogra, it would be the greatest benefit that could be conferred on the province. It may further be observed, that the extension of the system of granting *pattas* down to every one who holds land of another, which the Chief Commissioner has directed, will afford ample protection to every cultivator."

These were the instructions given by Sir Charles Wingfield with regard to the occupancy rights in Oudh. These words were turned and twisted in every possible direction by captious critics. We will see afterwards what complications were produced by these words, as soon as Lord Canning laid down the reins of Government. Suffice it to say here that Lord Canning thus gave his sanction to this para. in the following words:

"The Governor-General approves *generally* of your instructions (para. 31, Record of Rights) to make no distinction between cultivators on fixed rates of occupancy and cultivators-at-will" (January 8, 1861).

It will be seen that the Record of Rights insisted on the right of Government to take its share of half the gross rental of the land. The Governor-General directed the Chief Commissioner that care should be taken not to allow intermediate holders to absorb an undue share of the rental of an estate to the prejudice of the Government revenue. As a general rule, the principle that the Government was entitled to 50 per cent. of the gross rental, was in every case to be observed and acted up to; and out of the remaining 50 per cent. were to be defrayed the village expenses and the shares of the rent to which the taluqdars and the intermediate holders were respectively entitled.

The instructions contained in the Record of Rights "appeared to the Governor-General to be generally very just and proper, and to be framed in accordance with the views which the Government had already expressed."

With reference to para. 31 of the Record of Rights the Chief Commissioner was informed, that the Governor-General approved generally of his instructions to make no distinction between cultivators on fixed rates of occupancy and cultivators-at-will. Here we find that Sir Charles Wingfield had the sanction of Lord Canning to recognize no occupancy rights in Oudh. Sir Charles had, after a very careful enquiry, come to the conclusion that these alleged rights were a myth in Oudh. He was aware that the followers of the Thomasonian school had *created* such rights in the North-West, and the country had reaped a harvest of woe during the late disturbances. The Chief Commissioner entertained very strong views on this subject, and had to pay a severe penalty for his opinions. The vexed question of occupancy rights in Oudh has been sifted in every possible way, and the conclusions which Sir Charles Wingfield arrived at were repeatedly proved to be absolutely correct. It will be seen, as we proceed, what a storm was raised by Lord Lawrence in this province during his Viceroyalty, and how triumphantly Sir Charles Wingfield and his friends came out of the Oudh *imbroglio.* The conflict of opinion upon the occupancy question was exceedingly strong, and the animus which marked the discussion was of no ordinary character. Even now we cannot exactly say that the bitter feelings which were engendered at that time between the advocates of the rival systems have entirely died away. The swell of the wave is still seen from time to time to agitate the minds of our administrators. The theory of the Dead Level has struck its root so deep in the soil, that even the bitter experience of 1857 and the calm and deliberate opinions recorded by the saviour of India have not been able to shake its foundation. "There should be nothing between the prince and the peasant;" this doctrine, though its baleful consequences have been demonstrated to be fatal to the true interests of the people, is still swaying the policy of a certain class of statesmen. "To oust a taluqdar," as Sir John Kaye very pertinently said "was held by some young Settlement Officers to be as great an achievement as to shoot a tiger." That generation of Settlement Officers, we are glad to say, has passed away, but it has been succeeded by a generation which, imbibing the spirit of its predecessors, cavils at the wise and benevolent policy of Lord Canning, and tries to undo its effects. Even a hard rock, it is said, wears away by constant dripping; and the utterances of inexperienced and misguided politicians, though harmless at the present day, may, by their constant reiteration, prejudice the minds of people who are unacquainted with the past history of Oudh.

No distinction then was to be made in the records at the regular settlement between cultivators at fixed rates and cultivators-at-will. In other words, the right of permanent occupancy at an unvarying rent was not to be *created* in Oudh, as in the Punjab. Settlement Officers were instructed not to be led away by plausible theories, and to record only those rights which *actually existed,* and not those which existed only in the imaginations of would-be benefactors of India. If it was clearly proved that certain privileged persons enjoyed those rights, they were certainly to be protected, but they were to be on no account *created* in Oudh.

Sir George Campbell's Phantasy.

Things remained in this state till the question of occupancy rights was re-opened by Mr. (now Sir George) Campbell, the Judicial Commissioner of Oudh, in his Administration Report for 1860 :—" My own impression is," says Sir George Campbell, " that, under all tenures and all systems, in all parts of India, at the bottom of all a strong tenant right exists, which has survived everything in some districts in Lower Bengal, and in most other provinces, and that very much indeed depends on the maintenance of these indigenous rights of the masses. We now know even the serfs of Russia would not value freedom unless it were accompanied by some defined rights in the soil. I look on it as a great advantage of the large tenures of Oudh that the great holders are less likely to interfere with these rights of the tillers of the soil than petty landholders.

" But still questions between the superior holders and the privileged cultivators must arise; the rights of the latter have not been recorded or defined; and care must be taken that when the system now discussed further progresses, it does not give one class an unfair advantage over another."

On receiving this report, Mr. Yule, who officiated as Chief Commissioner in the absence of Sir Charles Wingfield, on leave, made diligent inquiries regarding the rights of cultivators adverted to by the Judicial Commissioner. Every taluqdar, however, to whom the Officiating Chief Commissioner spoke on the subject, denied the existence of any right on the part of cultivators of any description to hold land at fixed rates; they one and all declared that no such right was ever known in the province. Some officers of the Commission, however, believed in the existence here of a tenant right at fixed rates; but this belief, Mr. Yule opined, arose more from a feeling that, what then existed elsewhere in provinces to which they had been accustomed, must or should exist here, than from any precise knowledge of its actual existence.

The Judicial Commissioner, in forwarding his report for 1861, again touched on the question of tenant rights: "It appears," he said, "to be generally understood that, though there were in Oudh no cultivators at actual fixed rates, there certainly were cultivators possessing a right of occupancy and liable to regulated rates, by which right they were distinguished from tenants-at-will. The holding of the superior zemindars from Government was of the same nature, but less distinctly regulated. The British Government regulates its demand by fixed rates short of the utmost limit of demand. It is then for the Government to determine by its own laws whether the margin created by this limit is to be given exclusively to the superior holder, or is to be, in any degree, shared by the inferior holders; and at any rate it does seem that to permit under our strong rule (which destroys the right of resistance) such unlimited enhancement at the discretion of the zemindars as to render the ancient tenants in practice mere tenants-at-will, would put them in a decidedly worse position than they previously occupied.

"It may well be that it is most injurious rashly to create rights in waste land, or to render irremoveable persons who are really tenants-at-will; but if we avoid that error, we shall probably have a sufficient field to occupy capital and enterprise for some generations, without trenching on really existing rights. It may be also that we should find it equally an evil if we by any means reduce the whole of the cultivators to a dead level of rack-rented tenants-at-will before we have the enterprise and capital to occupy so large a field. Changes are best effected gradually, and we shall most safely, as well as most justly, follow the line of existing facts. It is clear that, as the country advances, great rent questions must arise between the superior and inferior holders; and I cannot but think that there is some ground for apprehending that if, while the rights of the latter are not recorded, the former are allowed for a series of years to decide cases which affect their own interests, the inferior rights may be obliterated more quickly than under ordinary circumstances they would have been."

Sir Charles Wingfield, who had now returned from leave, pointed out to the Governor-General that the inferences made by the Judicial Commissioner were wholly unwarranted, and were calculated to mislead. The Chief Commissioner never professed to ignore the existence of cultivators with rights of occupancy as distinct from mere tenants-at-will; but as he was convinced that there were no cultivators with rights of occupancy at fixed,—*i.e.*, unvarying rates, in Oudh,—he drew a broad line of separation, and did not think it necessary to particularize between cultivators with or without rights of occupancy. Indeed, he did not think the determination of this latter question and of what will hereafter constitute a fair rate of rent subjects for general investigation at settlement. To enter upon such an inquiry was sure to rouse a spirit of antagonism between landlord and tenant, who, if left to themselves, would rarely dispute at all.

Sir Charles Wingfield's views on the general question were briefly these:—"That although there are no cultivators in Oudh entitled to hold at fixed rates, there are cultivators with rights of occupancy, but this right cannot be made to depend on occupation of the land for *twelve* years, or any arbitrarily assumed period of time; nor does it restrict the landlord from raising the rent, after due warning, if other cultivators are ready to give more for the land than the present occupant pays; and if it is a fair rent and not an excessive one, run up merely to oust him. In short, the right of occupancy only entitles the tenant to hold at market-rates and protect him from wanton eviction."

Sir Charles Wingfield would on no account agree to introduce into Oudh the class known in the North-Western Provinces as '*maurasi*,' or cultivators with permanent rights of occupancy at fixed rates. They and the rights they were declared to possess were utterly unknown till the British Government created them.

As a consequence of this ill-advised procedure, many evils have resulted, and the value of the property has been materially impaired by the interference which was practised by the Government between landlord and tenant at the regular settlement in the North-Western Provinces.

There is not the least foundation for Mr. Campbell's assertion that there were under the native Government certain well-known and 'regulated' rates at which cultivators were entitled to hold in Oudh. Such established rates have in practice scarcely anywhere been found to exist. It can be easily proved that there was no limitation on the power of the landlord to raise the rent beyond what his own interest, which required that the land should not be left untilled, would impose on him.

Both Mr. Yule and Sir Charles Wingfield were firmly of opinion that the ryot or cultivator was merely entitled to *occupy* on payment of a fair rent, and that no period of occupation alone gave a right to hold at fixed rates, and that no ryot entering by virtue of a patta for a fixed period on the occupancy of land not before in his occupation had any right to occupancy after the period of his patta had expired. There might have been exceptional cases when the right of a mere ryot to hold at fixed rates was acknowledged to exist, but this right never took its rise in occupancy only, but always had some distinct recognizable origin. Such a rare and exceptional right had its origin in former proprietorship, all vestige of which has long since disappeared, except as far as it is preserved in the permission conceded by the present proprietors of holding a little land at favorable rates.

The Tenant-Right Question.

The tenant-right question assumed a new phase during the viceroyalty of Lord Lawrence. He enquired of Sir Charles Wingfield, the Chief Commissioner, whether, apart from the question whether right of occupancy implied a right to a fixed rate of rent, any measures have been taken for the recording of such rights, and whether, in fact, they were protected otherwise than by the jurisdiction of the Courts, or whether the Settlement

Officers had been directed not to make enquiries with a view to the record of this class of rights.

Sir Charles Wingfield said in reply, that the taluqdars could not and would not complain if the ryots were protected in any rights they might be found to possess; but he observed that, inasmuch as he was convinced that no such rights ever existed in Oudh, he had instructed the Settlement Officers not to record rights of occupancy at fixed rates by cultivators, and that no distinction between cultivators should be made in the settlement record. These instructions were issued by him with the general approval of Lord Canning.

Sir Charles Wingfield's Views.

In March 1864, Sir Charles Wingfield took a bolder attitude. In his letter, dated 15th December 1862, the Chief Commissioner had explained his views on the general question to be that, admitting a right of occupancy on the part of non-proprietary cultivators, this right could not be made to depend on any period of time, nor did it restrict the landlord from raising the rent after due warning, if others were ready to give more for the land than the present occupant paid. The right of occupancy he defined as entitling the tenant to hold at market-rates and as protecting him from wanton eviction; but the light that was thrown on this subject by personal enquiry, and the reports of the District and Settlement Officers induced the Chief Commissioner to believe that, under the influence of prepossessions acquired in the North-Western Provinces, he had made too hasty an admission; and the conviction was now forced on him that a right of occupancy in non-proprietary cultivators had never in theory or practice existed in Oudh. The enquiry made by Lord Lawrence, referred to above, precluded the discussion of the question of a right to hold at a fixed rate of rent, and it was not necessary for the Chief Commissioner to refer to it further, as he did not admit the lesser right of mere occupancy. It was indeed certain that there never was any such limitation on the powers of the landlord; and even the late Mr. Thomason, though he claimed it in favor of hereditary tenants in his directions to Settlement Officers, would appear to have very considerably modified that opinion in his printed despatches. The opinions of Commissioners and all the officers engaged in making settlement or in charge of districts, which Sir Charles Wingfield had called for, confirmed his view of the question; the great majority of them denied altogether the existence of a class of tenants with rights of occupancy. The information which the searching enquiry of Mr. Wingfield elicited served to establish the fact that many cultivators had held for generations under the same proprietary family, and that the feeling of all classes and, it may be added, the interests of the landlord were opposed to evicting an old tenant without cause in favour of a new one. It also showed clearly that no doubt ever existed in the mind of the people in regard to the landlord having the power to increase the rent or to eject a tenant at his pleasure; the same conditions may be found in England. On some great estates, farms have descended from father to son without written leases for two centuries, and though the landlord is naturally attached to an old hereditary tenantry and would deem it wrong to break the connection that subsisted so long, not one of them would venture to assert that his occupation for centuries gives him any interest in the land beyond that of a mere tenant-at-will. Much the same feeling influences the relation between master and servant, the borrower and lender, in this country, where service in landed families is generally hereditary. It may be said that in such a state of society as prevailed in Oudh, where there was no law but that of the strong, the non-existence of a right of occupancy is not to be assumed for want of its formal recognition. The Chief Commissioner would reply that had such a right ever existed, it would be found occasionally in vigour, or its traces would often be so unmistakeably apparent as to leave no room for difference of opinion on the subject. Though overborne for a time, it would have been kept alive in the hearts of the people as proprietary right had been.

So far from having been able to discover any trace of such a right, Sir Charles Wingfield could assert without fear of contradiction:

"*Firstly*, that every landholder has always exercised the right of ousting a ryot at his pleasure, which not even the ryot can deny. *Secondly*, that the local authorities and village punchayets under the native rule never interfered between the cultivator and owner of land, though these tribunals constantly adjudicated in claims to rights in land. *Thirdly*, that in the innumerable sepoys' petitions sent through the Residents at Lucknow, complaining of every manner of injustice, none but proprietary rights in land were laid claim to.

"The want of communication and markets for produce, which kept down prices, and the stagnation of every branch of industry, owing to the disorders of the administration and the turbulence of the people, would satisfactorily account for the somewhat stationary character of rents before Annexation; but practically the landlord did raise his rents by imposing contributions and cesses on his tenants on every conceivable pretext.

"Many of the Brahmins and Rajpoots possess, or have been admitted to, under-proprietary rights; and Circular No. 2 of 1861 shows that every form of proprietary right in the land, independent or acquired, has been carefully guarded; but those who are merely cultivators generally pay lower rates than other castes; superstition favored the former, and is likely to favor them for some time to come, as reverence for Brahmins, which is a marked feature in the character of Oudh landholders, will not rapidly decline. But instead of seeking to perpetuate privileges according to caste ascendency, the British Government should rather look forward with satisfaction to the time when caste will confer no advantages, and when Brahmins and Rajpoots will have lost the false pride that now makes them think it derogatory to put their hands to the plough, and compels the employment of servants to do the work of cultivators.

"The Rajpoot clansmen held at lower rates in return for military services. As the condition on which they enjoyed those privileges is no longer insisted on, the right to them ceases: the Government does not continue rent-free grants conditional on service to be performed when the service is no longer required, and it would be urged that we should not call on landholders to make greater sacrifices than we impose on ourselves.

"It must be admitted that both these classes will suffer from the change in the Government and the condition of society in

Oudh, but not to so great a degree as some other classes of the population. The Mahomedan residents of Lucknow and the other cities, who have lost employment by the withdrawal of the court, and in the Irregular Corps of the native Government, and have no land to fall back upon, are greater sufferers; and so are the Passees, whose occupation is also gone. And against the altered demeanour of the taluqdars to their clansmen and Brahmin tenantry, described by Mr. Tucker, the Chief Commissioner may set the testimony of Major Orr, of the late Oudh service, whose knowledge of the province exceeds that of any officer in the service of Government, who, in writing on another subject, and describing the destitution of the classes above-mentioned, remarked that the Brahmins and Rajpoots received their remuneration for service in the form of low rents, which are generally continued to them by the taluqdars. Such, as has already been said, is the influence of superstition that few of the present generation of landholders will dare to raise the rents of Brahmin cultivators to the level of what other castes pay; but it cannot be admitted that a right of occupancy existed in these any more than in other classes of cultivators, or that caste prejudices give a claim to privileges which must be denied to the humbler and more industrious races.

"The case has been put of tenants who have made wells, tanks, &c. Improvement of the land, no doubt, gives a claim to consideration, which will rarely be ignored; but, except on conditions agreed to by the landlord, it can give no right to occupy the land permanently, and to hold otherwise might have the effect of compelling landlords to interdict all improvements."

The Chief Commissioner has endeavoured to show, in the foregoing paras., that no right of occupancy or custom which has acquired the force of a right, can be proved on the part of the non-proprietary cultivators; and would, therefore, submit that none could be given them which would not be so much taken from the landlords. The sunuds that the taluqdars hold, only provided for the maintenance of the rights previously enjoyed, and they may fairly urge that it would be a violation of the guarantee if new rights be created to their prejudice. Apprehension (which the Chief Commissioner believes to be unfounded) of the landlord being tempted to abuse his power under a state of society that makes him less dependant on the good will of some of his tenantry the Chief Commissioner says 'some,' advisedly, because he believes the industrious classes of cultivators are more in demand than ever they were) would not, in his opinion, justify the Government in curtailing his rights.

The Chief Commissioner may, perhaps, be told that Oudh, which is peopled by the same races, cannot differ so much from the adjoining districts of the North-West Provinces, where rights of occupancy were recorded at the settlement of 1833. He is not prepared to admit that these rights had any better foundation in the North-West Provinces than he has been able to discover for them in Oudh. It is not too much to say that, when our Settlement Officers began their task, a strong re-action had set in against the principles of the Permanent Settlement, by which it was supposed that the interests of the peasantry had been unduly neglected. Moreover, during the thirty years of our rule that preceded their inquiries, the early Bengal Regulations, which recognized such rights in a part of the country where the proprietary status was widely different, had been in force, and new interests had, consequently, sprung up. That they were not so apparent to the earlier Revenue Officers, who must have possessed a clearer insight into the condition of the peasantry before the cession, may be gathered from Appendix 5 of 'Elphinstone's History of India,' wherein it is stated that, on a report called for by the Government in 1815, eleven out of fourteen Collectors in the North-West Provinces considered the landlord entitled to raise his rent or oust his tenant at pleasure, and that further enquiry tended to confirm this conclusion. The Chief Commissioner speaks from his own knowledge when he says that he has seen, in more than one district, rights of occupancy profusely and indiscriminately bestowed on peasants who had no claim to them.

The Chief Commissioner believes that the rights of occupancy recorded at the settlement in the North-West Provinces were a creation of our own; and this view is borne out not only by the above reports, but by reference to those of some of the Punjab Settlement Officers; and to a correspondence recently circulated by the Punjab Financial Commissioner, styled Proposed Tenant Code,' where the Chief Commissioner (Sir Charles Wingfield) finds numerous officers affirming in plain terms that the distinction between hereditary cultivators and tenants-at-will was unknown under the Sikh rule, and that the right of hereditary occupancy was entirely created by our Government, and, as the correspondence further shows, on arbitrary and varying rules.

Indeed, the Chief Commissioner would feel embarrassed if called upon to lay down any rule or principle for the determination of such rights. In the North-West Provinces a simple process was adopted of declaring every cultivator who had held the same land for twelve years possessed of a right of occupancy, and this rule has been embodied in Act X of 1859; but the Chief Commissioner apprehends that the inapplicability of such a test, or of any one founded on an arbitrarily assumed period of occupancy, without reference to its nature or origin, will now be conceded. The immediate effect might be to cause every landholder to eject all tenants who have held for less than the prescribed period; and one European landholder has intimated that, in self-defence, he must take this course if Act X of 1859 be introduced into Oudh. The Chief Commissioner confesses he does not see how any period of occupation can give a ryot, who has been settled on the estate by the landholder or his ancestors, a right to till the land against the owner's consent; he further submits that no ryot whose ancestors were settled on the estate can have, by mere lapse of time, acquired rights adverse to the landlord.

It should be here observed that the taluqdars, warned by the experience of the North-Western Provinces, and relying on their sunuds, might, perhaps, contest all such claims.

But supposing a right of occupancy be decreed to the ryot, the question next arises, what practical advantage will he derive from it? In the North-Western Provinces the right was valued, because it was always accompanied by the determination of his rent, and the limitation of the amount to the period of settlement. But, by the old Regulations and Act X of 1859, the rent of a tenant possessing rights of occupancy can be raised under certain circumstances; and the recent decision of the High Court in the Hill's case has laid down the law, even in Bengal, to be, that a ryot with rights of occupancy is not entitled to a share in the profits of the land, and has merely a right to occupy the land in preference to another at a fair rent; and what a fair rent is, competition alone can determine. The tenant, therefore, gains nothing by a right so defined, for no landlord wants to get rid of a tenant who will pay the market-rate for the land. The Chief Commissioner apprehends that the Courts will follow the law as laid down by the Chief Justice, and the end will only be that we shall give the ryot a barren privilege, which will, nevertheless, inspire him with vain hopes and provoke the opposition of the landlords, and thus create an antagonism of classes and swamp the Courts with fruitless litigation. In support of this position, the Chief Commissioner would refer the Government of India to the letter already quoted, No. 1007, dated 27th March 1849, in which the late Lieutenant-Governor of the North-Western Provinces, Mr. Thomason, expresses his belief "that disputes regarding the right of occupancy and rates seldom occur, except where the position of the tenants has been fixed by the operation of the existing revenue system." The Chief Commissioner hopes that, under such circumstances, it will be admitted that the right of occupancy, if decreed, would give the possessor no practical advantage over a tenant-at-will.

The Chief Commissioner would further submit, that the reports of the Bengal officers on the working of Act X of 1859, in the year 1862, which he has lately perused, present the strongest evidence of the hopelessness of attempting to control the relations of persons whose affairs can only be regulated by their own interests; indeed, it seems to Mr. Wingfield that it would be almost as impracticable for the Government to fix fair rents on the land as to determine equitable rates of payment for the necessaries of life.

Undoubtedly, we are bound, and should be prompt, to recognize existing rights, however hampering and opposed to the public welfare, and, as has been stated before, already ample provision has been made for the recognition of all and every claim which may be based on a proprietary right. But when no such right as that of occupancy of another man's land against his will can be proved to exist, which the Chief Commissioner submits to be the case, he would deem the creation of it impolitic; indeed, on every principle of upholding existing rights, the right of the landlord to get the best rent he can for his land should be respected. The relations between the hirer and the letter of land should, in the Chief Commissioner's opinion, be as unrestricted as between the buyer and seller of merchandize. The owner of land appears to him to have as much right as the owner of a house to let his property on the best terms, and any limitation of his power over it must tend to deter the application of capital to the land, and check the development of its productive powers, and, consequently, of the wealth of the country.

The claim of any interest, landed or commercial, to protection in its industry has been repudiated in England, but in India it is accorded to the lowest form of agricultural interest. This course of policy, the Chief Commissioner believes to be opposed to modern principles. The doctrine, that it is the duty of the State to interfere to prevent the owner of the soil from doing what he pleases with it, is one that Englishmen will not subscribe to in their own country;* every attempt to legalize it under the guise of tenant-right in Ireland has been defeated in Parliament, and the idea of limiting the power of the landlord as to the rent he may put on his land, or the choice of a tenant, has been denounced as communistic by an eminent living statesman.†

* This is not the case now, as my readers are aware.

† It would appear that the doctrines here referred to by Sir Charles Wingfield as the universal creed of Englishmen have been departed from in the case of recent legislation with regard to land in Ireland; and the agitation still being carried on in England and Scotland on the land question points to still further legislation in the same direction. It is to be observed, however, that the elements which, in these countries, go to form the chief factors in the situation are wanting in Oudh. In England and Scotland the large and prosperous urban populations have created a demand for food stuffs far in excess of that which the soil of the countries themselves can supply. Agricultural produce of all kinds could thus command extravagant prices, and the market-value of land rose correspondingly high. So long as this state of things lasted, the British farmer was the most prosperous of men. At the present time, however, the agricultural industry of England is paralyzed to a considerable extent on

The Chief Commissioner is aware of no reason why these principles, which he believes to be based on the natural laws of society and of political economy, should be inapplicable to India. He sees no ground for apprehension from agrarian outrages from giving effect to them; on the contrary, the Chief Commissioner has already attempted to demonstrate that the violation of these principles is the surest way of creating antagonism of classes, as the operation of Act X of 1859 has shown. The supposition that raising the rent lessens the peasant's means of subsistence is, in his opinion, erroneous; a rise in rents is the sign of increase in the value of produce, and, consequently, of progress in wealth and prosperity. Any measure that would keep rents down is injurious to the interests of all classes, and of none more than the cultivators themselves, to whom the stimulus to exertion and improvement would be wanting. The Chief Commissioner apprehends that if no rents were demanded from the Indian ryot, agriculture would deteriorate, and wealth and population decline. It being his view that every landlord is entitled to demand the market-rate for his land, it follows, in his opinion, that the tenant who does not pay it should take his labour elsewhere;

---

account of foreign competition, chiefly on the part of America. Without going into details it is sufficient to state, that agricultural produce can be imported into England from America and the Colonies and sold at prices lower than the rates at which home producers can supply the markets. As an immediate consequence of this, farmers are unable to pay the high rents they have hitherto given. Landowners, in the meantime, refuse to let their land at lower rents, persuading themselves that the depression is only temporary. Farmers are thus obliged either to yield to the landlords' demands or to quit the land. The latter alternative, if carried out on a large scale, would obviously lead to a social revolution. It can thus be seen how a particular combination of circumstances has, in England, led up to a point where legislative interference may become necessary. In Ireland, where, owing to the peculiar nature of the existing land-tenure, and to the fact that rack-renting has long prevailed there, the people began to feel the pressure of events earlier, the law has already stepped in. It would be folly to argue that, because Government has interfered in Ireland between landlord and tenant, it must necessarily do the same thing in Oudh, irrespective of the circumstances which call for interference. It will readily appear from the short resumé of facts above given, that the condition of Oudh is in no respect analagous to that of those countries where the land quesion has just come to the front; and that, consequently, they supply us with no parallel for similar action here.

so far from training the ryot in the idea that he has a right to till the same soil as his forefathers, the wiser and kinder policy would be to encourage him to take his labour to the best market, for it is the clinging to the soil, fostered by our system, which retards the reclamation of the waste lands, and impedes the progress of European enterprise.

It is well known that there is no superfluity of labour in India, though it is redundant in parts. If all the land in Oudh once cultivated, but for many years abandoned, were brought under the plough, the province would support another million or more of people. This consideration was before the Chief Commissioner when he drew up his circulars, in which the creation of cultivators at fixed rates was interdicted.

Since then there are no rights of occupancy, it will be as impossible for the ordinary Revenue Courts, as for the Settlement Officers, to say who is possessed of them, and yet it must be confessed that the original plan of leaving this question to the decision of the District Courts is inconsistent and impracticable. He (the Chief Commissioner) would, therefore, confine the jurisdiction of the Courts, in suits between landlord and tenant, to breaches of contract,—*i. e.*, breaches of the terms of the leases and complaints of ouster in the midst of the agricultural year, when no tenant should be ejected except upon default.

The Chief Commissioner is convinced that the condition of the ryot in Oudh will not thus be made much worse than that of the non-proprietary cultivator in the provinces where he is favored by exceptional legislation, for the interests of the landlord will be his best protection here, as in point of fact they were found to be in the North-Western Provinces (*vide* para. 126 of "The Directions to Settlement Officers").*

The condition of the ryot under the native Government was, no doubt, precarious, but it was not by the landlord demanding too high a rent, as any one who knew Oudh will testify, but

* Non-proprietary cultivators are generally either the descendants of former dispossessed proprietors, or they have been located on the estate by the present proprietors or their predecessors; their best security, no doubt, consists in the demand for their labour. A zemindar commonly reckons his wealth by the number of his *assamees*, and the fear of losing their services is sufficient provision against harshness or severity towards them.

by his taking more than had been agreed on, that the ryot was subject to exaction under the native rule; the landlord could not raise his rent to an excessive amount, because, if he had, the cultivator would rather have gone elsewhere than pay it; he, therefore, waited till the harvest was ripe before he commenced his exactions. From oppressions of this kind, our Courts, which bind both parties to the engagements entered into, will effectually protect the ryot. The Chief Commissioner believes that even now the cases in which real non-proprietary cultivators go into the Summary Suit Court against their landlords, are very rare; under-proprietary claims underlie, if they do not form the ground of the majority of the suits.

As sound policy has been adduced as a reason for recognizing rights of occupancy on the part of cultivators, the Chief Commissioner may, perhaps, be allowed to treat the question in a purely political point of view. No one of course would ask that the support of any one class should be gained by the sacrifice of the rights of another, but there are many who think that the security of our empire in the east depends on the attachment of the mass of the peasantry. The Chief Commissioner confesses he differs from them, and deems it to be only his duty to avow his opinion, that, in the attachment of the landed aristocracy, more effective support of our rule could be found; the utter inability, even if there were the will, on the part of the peasantry to help us was, the Chief Commissioner thinks, unmistakably evinced during the late disturbances; where the land was in the hands of the peasants, the flames of insurrection and rapine spread unchecked; they were arrested only when they reached the territories of some independent prince or great proprietor. Of the truth of this assertion, he could adduce numerous instances, but they must have presented themselves to everyone who has had experience of those times. What made the insurrection in Oudh so formidable was, that the aristocracy of the land placed themselves at its head. The same remark applies in a less degree to the rebellion of Behar. The Chief Commissioner is not aware of one instance where the peasantry remained loyal when the taluqdars went into revolt; they invariably followed the lead of their hereditary chief.

Those English officials whose fate it was to wander as fugitives during the Mutiny heard many truths which in other times would never have reached their ears; and the Chief Commissioner can say from experience that our system which has led to the decay of the ancient landed families in the North-West Provinces, was often regarded with dislike, even by the peasantry whom we had raised on their ruins, but who nevertheless saw with regret the extinction or impoverishment of ancient families, which they revere as the heads of their race.

The Chief Commissioner, therefore, holds that the policy most conducive to our interests is to secure the attachment of the landed aristocracy when we are so fortunate as to possess one that consists of the hereditary chiefs of the country; and, with few exceptions, the taluqdars of Oudh answer to that character. We give the peasantry the benefit of equal laws, and should relieve them from every restriction that can hamper their industry, but we ought not to give them what belongs to others. No doubt, they will be gratified by being told that the property in the land belongs in part to them, and that the owner may not lease it to others, or take what rent he can get for it; but while by this course we alienate the landed gentry, the Chief Commissioner cannot admit that the future contenment and prosperity of the peasantry will be secured by it. On the contrary, he thinks their prosperity and that of future generations is most likely to be promoted by emancipating them from the idea that they are bound to the soil on which they are born, by teaching them to rely on their own exertion to better their condition, and to seek the wide fields of industry open to them, and by giving free scope to the ordinary laws of social progress.

The Chief Commissioner forwarded also a short abstract of the opinions of Commissioners and officers engaged in settlement work, regarding the existence of an hereditary tenant-right. It was as follows:—

"Mr. Currie (Commissioner of Settlement), Major Chamier, Captains MacAndrew and Thompson, Messrs. King, Anderson, Glynn, and Kavanagh (Deputy Commissioners and Officiating Commissioners) are of opinion, that there is no class of non-proprietary cultivators possessing rights of occupancy distinct from tenants-at-will.

"Mr. Young, Assistant Commissioner in charge of Fyzabad District throughout 1863, says that, in summary suits, cultivators may plead that they and their ancestors have tilled the land for generations, and this is the case, but always at variable rents. No right of occupancy was ever respected by the landholder, nor has he ever seen a right of occupancy claimed apart from proprietary claims of some kind or other.

"Mr. Simpson, Commissioner, Fyzabad Division, thinks we did find at Annexation rights of occupancy existing in a certain class of cultivators, but that these rights were fostered by the landlords from motives of self-interest, and did not derive their sanction from any law, or usage having the force of law, and the right merely conferred a right to occupy the land in preference to any other tenant without necessarily involving more favorable terms as regards rent. That many cultivators are to be found, according to Mr. Simpson, all over the province, who have cultivated the same field for years, is a well-known and undoubted fact; but in a country under a Government, such as that of Oudh was for many years previous to Annexation, it were vain to expect to find any law, or usage having the force of law, sanctioning this custom, and its growth and prevalence are due, in his opinion, to the character of the times in which it obtained. Mr. Simpson, speaking of the different stages of division of the property in land, says (quoting from an article in the *Friend of India*, September 1863):—'The second stage is to divide the property in land between the cultivating rent-payer and the protecting rent-receiver. As long as society remains in a lawless and insecure state, this divided property in the land works well, because it is the natural expression of the best understood interests of both. This is the feudal state of landed tenures. The lord affords protection to his vassals, who, in return, pay him suit and service as well as rent, and form his only defence against his enemies. The vassals pay such surplus of their produce as is necessary for the maintenance of the lord and his more immediate retainers, because such payment is the very condition of the lord's continued power to protect them; and the lord grants his vassals permanent rights in their holdings, and does not stretch his demand to their utmost ability to pay, because the attachment and willing support of his vassals against his enemies is more important to him than a mere increased receipt of produce in kind.' From his reference to a feudal state of society, and by the important qualifications he adds to his description of a pre-annexation occupancy right, Mr. Simpson would seem to reduce it to a minimum. His remark, therefore, that 'at Annexation, we did find rights of occupancy existing in a certain class of cultivators,' can only refer to Rajpoots and Brahmins, as they were the only classes that rendered military service as feudal retainers.

"Mr. Clifford, Deputy Commissioner, Oonao, alludes only to a right of occupancy at easy rates claimed by *mokuddums*, or head ryots, but explains that the privileges they enjoyed were in return for services in managing the villages and were not always hereditary; that the landlord could, if he pleased, dispense with their services, and employ other persons.

"Mr. Carnegy, Deputy Commissioner of Fyzabad, says, he does not think we have come across any cultivators whose connection with the soil can be said to constitute a right of occupancy as distinguished from tenants-at-will. He then describes certain persons who possess certain privileges. The first class corresponds with the *mokuddums* described by Mr. Clifford; the second had improved the land in their occupation; the third had reclaimed land from waste. These two classes in consequence pay lighter rates. Waste land was frequently given on clearing leases or on *birt* tenure, which conferred a proprietary right. Such tenures will be maintained as subordinate proprietary rights.

"Mr. Capper, Deputy Commissioner of Lucknow, names certain races,—'Lodh, Koormees, Kachees,'—as possessed of a cottier right of cultivation. This description of their condition I really cannot follow, or understand how their making common cause with the zemindars against the Government officials, or the tendency of their position to assimilate itself to that of serfs in Norman England and Russia, affords any evidence of the rights of occupancy now referred to.

"Mr. Capper, says the Settlement Commissioner, has launched out into an essay on imaginary rights of occupancy instead of confining himself to a concise reply to the questions submitted to him. His conclusions do not appear to me to be borne out by his premises. It is undoubtedly true that there are a certain class called '*chupperbund assamees*'; that these *assamees* are generally Aheers, Lodhs, Koormees or Moraees; that dispossessed zemindars chiefly directed their dacoities against these; and it was when these were driven out that they were enabled to recover possession. But all this proves nothing more than that it was the interest of the landowner to retain these men as tenants, because they were the best cultivators, and he could not replace them if they left him, while it was equally the interest of the dispossessed zemindar to endeavour to drive these men from the village, because if they went, the landowner in possession was obliged to go also. When the Settlement Officer comes to describe these *chupperbund assamees*, he is obliged to draw upon his imagination and refer to Aryan dynasties, the Emperor Akber's Doomsday Book, Sclave cultivators of Germany, and serfs of Russia. The long and short of his story being that, as long as these cultivators could be induced to remain in a village, their rent was liable to yearly adjustment according to the necessities of the landlord, and when it got too high to be endured, the cultivators, their rights of occupancy notwithstanding, bolted. The only right which I can discover from Mr. Capper's letter that these cultivators enjoyed, was the right of being rack-rented, if that can be called a right; and I can hardly understand how the non-recognition of this right can be deemed 'unjust,' according to native ideas, or cause a 'heart-breaking wrenching from the soil.'*

* It is but fair to quote here the exact words of Mr. Capper, so that the reader might compare them with Sir Charles Wingfield's remarks, and draw his own conclusions on the subject:

"That there are and were a class of '*chupperbund assamees*,' considered by all to have a cottier right of cultivation, I have never entertained a doubt. These are generally Aheers, Lodhs, Koormees, and Moraees, who, I doubt not, were often descendants of the original settlers before the successive waves of Brahmin, Rajpoot, and Mussalman invasion had destroyed all trace of their proprietary tenure in the soil.

"Mr. Boulderson, the Assistant Officer referred to by Mr. Capper, explains that cultivators had complained to him of being ejected

---

"Anyhow, these men, cultivating with their own hands, and content with their small profits, were the men on whom the conquering races chiefly relied for profits; and to this day villages are valued, not by area or soil, but by the number of cultivators of these classes who are permanent residents of the soil.

"It was against them that the dacoities of dispossessed zemindars were chiefly directed, and it was when the dispossessed Brahmin or Rajpoot proprietor could induce or terrify these men into taking to the jungle, that he was enabled to recover possession, owing to the failure of the new occupant to supply their place by emigration from other villages.

"As to their rights one cannot say: the different fields are generally still known by names given to them by their ancestors, which the Aryan and Mussalman proprietors cannot now interpret, and they at most invariably cultivate the best soils, and alone raise the best kinds of crops on those fields to which, by proximity to the village site, manure can be more easily conveyed.

"The mode of fixing their rent for the year appears to have been that, taking as a basis some traditionary jumma of the village, probably that village tradition of what was recorded in the Emperor Akbar's Doomsday Book, any increase was borne ratably; and in the latter days, when rent was by Government screwed up to the highest pitch, the only limit to the demand was the lowest amount that would leave bare subsistence to their families.

"If this was exceeded they bolted, and the malgoozar was ruined, and the greater part of the jumma had to be reduced, the village being '*becheragh* and *wairan*,' and then they gradually returned to their old homes to be screwed up again till the pressure became again intolerable.

"Had it not been for this common bond of union between them and the zemindars against the oppression of the sovereign and the Government servants, I have no doubt but that they would have occupied the precise position of the old Sclave cultivators of Germany, the serfs of Old Norman England and of the Russia of the present day.

"But except a taluqdar's agent, I do not think that any one will in quiet conversation deny their existence, and they have an undefined right to cultivate certain fields, which they have cultivated for generations at rates proportionate to the Government demand on the village, although these rates will generally, owing to their cultivating the best lands, be higher than those '*pykhast* cultivators,' who are tempted by lower rates to settle.

"The tendency of their holding, however, being to serfdom, I do not advocate recognition of the right in the present settlement.

"It will doubtless be unjust in native idea to ignore them; it will doubtless cause many a heart-breaking wrenching from the soil to which they have a more than cat-like affection; but they are the chief body to whom we can look for the permanent formation, *first*, of a class of field labourers working for wages, and *secondly*, of a class of landholding yeomanry; and if individuals suffer now, their descendants will prosper, as once disconnected from the soil of their birth, they have all the qualities which must bring them to the top, and though screwed by the spendthrift will always be tempted by liberal terms to emigrate to the lands of more careful landowners."

from fields they had cultivated for centuries (does not enter into the general question).

"Mr. Perkins, Deputy Commissioner of Sultanpore, says, that if an answer is to be given to the broad question, he would say that there is no class of cultivators possessed of permanent rights of occupancy. He goes on to remark that land has been held for several generations in one family, but it never occurred to cultivator or landlord to speculate on the existence or nature of the right enjoyed by either. In times past, the proprietor was more dependent on a good cultivator than he is at present. The tenant became attached to the land which then, as a matter of convenience, was transmitted from father to son. Therefore it cannot be denied that, though no prescriptive right is considered to rest in the tenant, public opinion among all classes of the community is opposed to the ejectment of a hereditary cultivator.

"Mr. Tucker, Commissioner, Khyrabad Division, assumes such right to exist, and recommends "that the landlord be restricted in his demands from all cultivators who have been in possession of the land for twelve years to the rental to be prescribed by the Settlement Officers, which should not exceed double the Government assessment."

Mr. Tucker's letter was dated 21st November 1861,—when Mr. Yule officiated as Chief Commissioner, during the absence of Mr. Wingfield on leave. Mr. Yule agreed with Mr. Tucker as to the absolute necessity of upholding existing rights; but considered that it would he the gravest infringement of that principle if he were to assume that because a man had rented a field from its owner at the same annual sum for twelve successive years, he was, therefore entitled to rent it for ever at the same sum, or at double the amount of a demand which Government, for the public interests, had fixed arbitrarily as the limit of its own right for a longer or shorter period, perhaps for ever. The owner of land is entitled to fair, that is, to the market-rates, for it (provided of course he has not contracted for others), as much as any merchant is entitled to the bazar price of his commodities, and this right to demand a higher rate when the market rises is not restricted by the fact of the market-rate having hitherto remained steady in consequence of small demand or other reasons arising from the state of society and Government. Had Mr. Yule found that such a right existed as that Mr. Tucker refers to, he would certainly have upheld it; but he never saw an instance of it, or even found an officer who could show him one.

Consultation at Cawnpore.

Sir Charles Wingfield met the Governor-General at Cawnpore in April 1864, when His Excellency explained to him his views on the settlement then in progress in Oudh. The Governor-General wished that the position of the non-proprietary cultivators should be defined, and those who had held for a *certain* time should be recorded as possessing a right of occupancy, and their rents fixed for the term of settlement.

Reference to the Taluqdars.

Sir Charles Wingfield, on his return to Lucknow, sent for about eight or ten of the most intelligent and influential taluqdars from different parts of the province, and informed them of the contemplated measures. With regard to the record of any non-proprietary cultivators, as possessed of a right of occupancy and to the limitation of the rent to be demanded from them during the term of settlement, the taluqdars, one and all, were most decidedly opposed to such a step, because they maintained that such rights had ever been unknown in this province, and their creation would strip them of the character of landlords and leave them a mere rent-charge on their estates. It was urged that non-proprietary cultivators in Oudh never possessed any such rights as are presumed to be vested in them, and to create them now would be an infringement of the terms of the *sunuds*, which only bound the taluqdars to the maintenance of existing rights. Such interference, it was submitted, between landlord and tenant would be detrimental to the best interests of all classes, and fatal to the progress and prosperity of the province. The difficulties that beset the course which it was proposed to pursue in Oudh were clearly pointed out to the Government of India. The taluqdars of Oudh, who had seen the effects of the creation of the rights of occupancy, and of fixing the rates of rent in the North-Western Provinces, would never be brought to consent to the admission of privileges destructive of their complete right of property in their estates. This complete title they naturally prized above all things, and, therefore, they would equally oppose, in the Courts of the provinces, a right of occupancy unaccompanied by determination of the rent.

Sir Charles Wingfield ventured to ask the Governor-General to take into serious consideration the effect that might be produced on the minds, not only of the people of this province, but of the upper classes throughout India, if the rights solemnly guaranteed to the taluqdars in open Durbar in the name of Her Majesty should be infringed. It was hardly too much to say that their confidence in the promises of their rulers, and in the stability of any course of policy, would be seriously shaken.

"The taluqdars," said the Governor-General, "affirm, that no such rights formerly existed in Oudh, and to this extent their statement may be true. Where a chief or man of influence had the power, he did what was good in his eyes. He cared neither for rights nor interests. But, on the other hand, where the tenant or village proprietor belonged to a clan, or a large body of agriculturists, the chief was made to respect his rights. But, as a rule, there were two strong points in favor of the people. Land was plentiful, and tenants were scarce; and thus the latter had some consideration. These men were a source of power to the leading chiefs, who could not maintain their position without such assistance. Under our rule, the great desire will be to accumulate money; and so the under-tenants will fare badly if left to the mercies of the proprietor.

"I do not desire to *create* rights in the land in Oudh; all I require is, that the rights which flow from long possession by general consent among the people shall be recognized and recorded.* Such rights any just native rule would admit; such rights our laws in India have distinctly laid down."

---

* It will be evident to a careful observer, that if tenants held their land for successive generations through the generosity or good feeling of the landlord, the Governor-General would thus be punishing the landlord for his patriarchal virtues.

"I quite subscribe to the doctrine," said Sir Charles Wingfield, "that the pledges given by Lord Canning and conveyed in the sunuds will not be infringed by maintaining any existing rights. It is on the existence of such rights on the part of non-proprietary cultivators that the issue turns. This the taluqdars and I also venture to deny, and I can assure your Excellency that I have not come to this conclusion without much enquiry and reflection. Perhaps had I remained in the North-Western Provinces, I should never have arrived at it, but here I have been brought face to face with native society in its unadulterated state, and with no other wish than to learn the truth, I have been unable to discover any trace of tenant-rights."

"The taluqdars," continued Sir Charles Wingfield, "are thoroughly resolved not to consent to the record of tenants with rights of occupancy at fixed rates, on the ground, as I have already stated, that no such rights ever existed, and to create them would be an infraction of the terms of the sunuds.

"The effect of such a measure would be to reduce enormously the value of their property. The highest rent that could now be fixed will not, probably, twenty years hence be half the average rate for land open to competition; so great a rise in prices or fall in the value of money may, I think, be anticipated from the agencies now at work; and this sacrifice will, I fear, be imposed on the landlords for the benefit of no one, for the rent the landlord loses will not enrich the tenant. With no motive for exertion he will be idle, and the country will be so much the poorer.

"Your Excellency will believe me when I say that if I thought that I was driving the non-proprietary peasantry of Oudh to misery, by refusing to confer on them rights of occupancy, I would be the first to urge the taluqdars to make concessions. But I have already expressed my belief that we shall best consult their future interests by non-interference between them and their landlords. There may be discontent on the part of the descendants of dispossessed proprietors and the clansmen who held at low rates on condition of military service. These are the classes who have the least claims on our sympathies, and protection will, I fear, convert them into lazy and useless middlemen.

But the cultivators of other races are, I am convinced, perfectly contented with their present condition, and on some estates, that of the Maharaja of Bulrampore for instance, enjoy a degree of happiness and comfort to which the peasantry of the North-Western Provinces are, I suspect, strangers, because the landlord not being afraid of their encroaching on his rights can afford to deal liberally with them, and no class antagonism arises."

Lord Lawrence's first Minute on the Tenant-Right Question.

The Governor-General wrote on the 20th of June 1864 an elaborate minute on this vexed question:—"The question now is," he asks, "what is the proper course to pursue? The Chief Commissioner affirms that no such rights as those which have been described exist in Oudh. My belief is that no sufficient enquiry has been made; and that the parties who claim such rights have not been allowed a hearing. In fact, the Chief Commissioner assumes that (in the Record of Rights), which should be the subject of investigation. The officers employed on the settlement operations show that tenant-rights of various kinds do exist in public opinion, and that a hearing is not allowed."

In the opinion of the Governor-General, the Bengal Revenue Regulations generally, and in particular Regulations VII of 1822 and IX of 1833, as well as Acts X of 1859 and XIV of 1863, should be introduced into Oudh.

Opinions of the Members of the Governor-General's Council.

The question was warmly discussed in the Council:—"The course which I would recommend," said Sir Henry Maine, "is simply to take issue with the taluqdars on the question they have raised. Let us for the first time have a full and free enquiry whether these rights exist. I would strike out from the Record of Rights, and from the instructions to Settlement Officers generally, so much as expresses any opinion of the existence or expediency of these rights—so much as appears to discourage their recognition—and so much as prohibits their being recorded. No ques-

Sir Henry Maine.

tion of good faith with the taluqdars is involved in such a course of proceeding; they do not urge that, if the hereditary tenants existed, we promised to abolish them; they merely assert their non-existence. I would, therefore, take every pains to convince the taluqdars that the inquiry is perfectly unbiased, and I would avoid the smallest appearance of antecedently assuming the existence in Oudh of beneficial occupancy.

"It will be seen that I venture to dissent from the Governor-General on the question of introducing into Oudh the Bengal Revenue Regulations and Act X of 1859. All these laws assume the existence of hereditary cultivators, and probably, according to the better opinion, of hereditary cultivators with beneficial rights; but I am most anxious not to make any antecedent assumption as to the existence of such a class in Oudh. Further, Act X, through the operation of the section which crowns a twelve years' possession with the right of occupancy, contains a machinery for creating hereditary cultivators, whether previously known in Oudh or not. To put such machinery into motion seems to me an act of injustice to the taluqdars, if not a breach of faith. Just as we expect them to recognize old rights of occupancy, if proved to exist, so we should abstain from encumbering their estates with new rights confessedly non-existent heretofore. It should be remembered, too, that the taluqdars can defeat the operation of the section by wholesale ejectments of every tenant-at-will who has not been in possession for twelve years. The evil of exposing them to such a temptation I need not dwell upon.

"I think that every pledge given directly by the Government of India to any person or class of persons should be religiously respected. I would, therefore, hold the obligations of the sunuds to be sacred.

"As a matter of policy, I most fully admit the inexpediency of abrupt recoils from one line of action to another. Knowing as we do how much the influence of this Government over the races which it rules depends on their impression of the stability and consistency of the principles which guide it, we must allow that it would be most unwise in the Government of India as constituted, during one of five years, rashly and on the score of any trivial difference of opinion, to break the thread of connection which unites it to the Government of the five years which precede it. One reason for my preferring the course which I have suggested to that which the Governor-General recommends is, that it does not appear to me to amount, on the face of it, to so open a departure from Lord Canning's policy"

Mr. Taylor.

"The question for decision is," said Mr. Taylor, "whether there are or are not hereditary tenants in Oudh who are entitled to hold their lands on certain advantageous terms. It is obviously desirable that the officer entrusted with the enquiry, and with the control of the settlement operations, should be as free from bias in one direction as in the other.

"In our future proceeding every care should, I think, be taken to guard against error in the opposite direction, namely, to attempt to create any sort of right or interest in the soil which does not now exist and has never existed. The assumption, either directly or by implication, of the existence of hereditary cultivators with beneficial rights should be as carefully avoided as the contrary assumption that they are unknown."

Sir Charles Trevelyan.

Sir Charles Trevelyan was of opinion that "all the subordinate rights in the land, *i.e.*, the rights which may exist between the taluqdar and the mere tenant-at-will, should be carefully investigated and equitably fixed and recorded"

Mr. Grey.

"It is my purpose," said Mr. Grey in his able Minute of 23rd September 1864, "to confine myself very much to a short statement of what I conceive to be the actual position of the case, as I gather it from the records, saying only as to the essential point at issue, that I entirely concur in the view taken by the Chief Commissioner, Mr. Wingfield, and the Settlement Commissioner, Mr. Currie; and that, having carefully read the reports of the District Officers and the Settlement Officers submitted to Government with Mr. Wingfield's letter of the 26th March, I am unable to agree in the conclusion drawn from those reports by the Governor-General and by Sir Charles Trevelyan. Indeed, it really seems to be not too much to say that, so far from those reports proving that tenant-rights of various kinds do exist, the only officers who seek to uphold that theory have written reports that are more calculated to discredit the theory than to establish it. I would refer specially to Mr. Capper's and Mr. Tucker's reports. The latter officer indeed can hardly be claimed as a supporter of the theory, for though he certainly urges the claim of the 'idle Rajpoots,' as he calls them, to hold their land on easy terms, he scarcely attempts to do so as a matter of right, but rather on grounds of policy. He urges that the privileges heretofore allowed to the idle Rajpoots by the landholders should be 'for a time at least' secured to them by the Government; not, he adds, that he is 'an advocate for granting privileges to the idle,' but that he thinks 'a paternal Government must treat with tenderness the shortcomings of its subjects, and that it cannot at once expect those who have never learnt to labour to perform as much work as those who have been accustomed from childhood to constant drudgery,' meaning the industrious Koormees and other low caste cultivators whose cause he does not advocate. He seems to intend that the Government, and not the taluqdars, should bear the cost of the indulgence he would extend to the 'idle Rajpoots,' for he suggests that the Government should assess lightly the lands held by these privileged classes, so as to induce the assent of the taluqdars to the course proposed. The best considered report seems to me to be that of Mr. Simpson, who in the end comes to much the same conclusion as Mr. Wingfield,—*viz.*, that while it may be true that old cultivators have a right of preference in the occupation of the land they have long cultivated, they have no right to demand that it shall be given to them at a cheaper rate than it is worth to other ryots.

"I deduce then from these reports the conclusion that there is no ground for the general theory put forward by Mr. Campbell, that there are ryots in Oudh with occupancy rights entitling them to pay rent at certain favorable and regulated rates; and it is because I think that it is really the setting up of this general theory, which is now sought, and not an enquiry into individual rights susceptible of being substantiated by tangible proof, that I attach weight to what has already been done, and consider that the deliberate action of a former Government in the matter should not be reversed.

"I proceed then to state briefly how the case appears to me to stand, being quite unable to agree in what I infer from expressions in His Excellency's minute to be the view of the Governor-General that the question is entirely an open one, on which the Government of the day is free to take any course it may deem best. I quite subscribe to the general principle enforced by Mr. Maine in his minute; but on the other hand I think, as regards the especial case under consideration, that very strong grounds should be shown for reversing the line of action deliberately taken by the Governor-General with reference to a province situated as Oudh was situated in 1858-59. I cannot think that the Governor-General takes a correct view of the sunud given to the taluqdars when he deduces from its words that it expressly reserved the rights of the cultivators, meaning thereby the general right of old cultivators to occupy the land on favorable terms. The words of the sunud cannot, in my opinion, be truly construed as including the question of occupancy rights of cultivators, by which I mean that it cannot be shown that the words were intended to include such cases, and consequently they could have been so understood by the taluqdars. This seems to me to be quite conclusively established if the letter of Government is referred to by which the revised sunud was sent to Mr. Wingfield. This letter is dated 19th October 1859. It referred expressly to the words quoted by the Governor-General requiring that all persons holding an interest in the land under the taluqdars shall be secured in the possession of subordinate rights which they have heretofore enjoyed, and it then proceeded to explain those words in the following manner:—'The meaning of this is, that when a regular settlement of the province is made, whenever it is found that zemindars or other persons have held an interest in the soil intermediate between the ryot and the taluqdar, the amount payable by the intermediate holder to the taluqdar will be fixed and recorded; and the tenor of the following paras. of the letter

(5 and 6) also clearly indicates that what was being spoken of and what was intended to be guarded by the sunud were under-proprietary rights and not occupancy rights of cultivators.' The actual position of the case then it appears to me to be stated as follows:—

"*1st.*—That Mr. Wingfield declared and reported his conviction to Government that no general right existed on the part of the cultivators in Oudh, whether the old indigenous low-caste ryots or the Brahmin and Rajpoot ryots, to hold the land under what is called a beneficial tenure,—that is to say, paying a lower rent for it than other ryots would generally be willing to pay for it.

"*2nd.*—That this condition of the case was accepted and confirmed by the then Governor-General Lord Canning.

"*3rd.*—That, accordingly, the sunud given to the taluqdars conferring on them the heritable and transferable proprietorship of their estates did not contain, and was not meant to contain, any reference to such a right.

"*4th.*—That the sunud so issued was approved by the Secretary of State.

"*5th.*—That it is now proposed,—in consequence of a statement made by Mr. Campbell in his annual report on the judicial administration to the effect that he believed the ryots in Oudh were entitled to hold the land at certain regulated rates, by which expression he meant rates according to some defined proportion of the produce,—to re-open and investigate afresh the question as to the general rights of the cultivator of Oudh.

"All that I desire to say on the point is, that, having carefully and to the best of my ability examined the circumstances of the present case, I cannot feel satisfied that sufficient ground is shown for questioning the decision which was come to by Lord Canning.

"I would add, that whatever doubt may be held to exist as to the possession of a beneficial right of occupancy by the ryots in more ancient times, it does appear to me to be quite beyond doubt that, under the native Government which was superseded by us, no such right was enjoyed, and that all the privileges which any cultivators possessed, such for instance as that enjoyed by the 'idle Rajpoots,' were only what was allowed by the landholders in their own interests and for their own advantage.

"Therefore it seems to me that, if Mr. Campbell's theory shall now prevail, we shall unquestionably be creating a right, so far at all events as the present generation of cultivators are concerned, and that we shall be creating such right in derogation of the right which was bestowed upon the taluqdars by Lord Canning in 1859."

Lord Lawrence's reply.

The Governor-General, in his Minute dated 27th September 1864, said in reply,—"that there is no need to advert to the interpretation which may have been placed on the wording of the sunud by various authorities. Its phraseology is most cautious and general. It provides that all holding under the taluqdars shall be secured in all the subordinate rights they *formerly enjoyed;* the real question therefore is, do the rights in question exist or not? Mr. Grey answers in the negative, basing his opinion on the reports of Mr. Wingfield, Mr. Currie, and the Settlement Officers. I see no reason for any deviation from the simple and open procedure followed in other provinces whereby those claiming rights of any sort are required to bring their cases before the officers deputed to hear them, and to abide by the decisions given on a consideration of the facts proved. If these rights can be investigated without any breach of the sunud, and if no sufficient investigation of them has yet been made, it is the bounden duty of Government to provide for them a fair hearing."

Sir Hugh Rose's Minute.

The Minute by Sir H. Rose, the Commander-in-Chief, is short and to the point:—"I am," he says, "as may be readily supposed, not master of this purely civil question; but an attentive perusal of the minute leads me as a member of the Government of the late Viceroy, Earl Canning, to say, that I should regret and deprecate the concession of tenant-rights, of whatever nature they may be, not sanctioned by law or equity to any inhabitants which are in conflict with or compromise the rights granted formally and officially to the taluqdars, &c., by Lord Canning's Government. I should regret it the more if such a concession, not based on positive right, affected a great and, I venture to think, a wise feature of his Lordship's policy—the maintenance of an Indian aristocracy, an useful link between the Government and the ignorant masses, which enables the former to obtain an insight into and control the feelings and passions of the people.

"Oudh, from having been the most turbulent, is now one of the most tranquil provinces in India. It would be a matter of regret, if inquiry, which might prove unnecessary, into tenant rights in Oudh—and there is no such fertile source of agrarian agitation and discontent as contested tenant-rights—were to disturb the propitious calm of one of the influential positions of India."

CHAPTER III.

THE INVESTIGATION.

Now, Sir Charles Wingfield was informed (September 30, 1864) that the Governor-General was of opinion that, as regards the occupancy rights of ryots, there was no room for the assertion that the recognition of cultivating rights, provided their existence was judicially established, involved any departure from Lord Canning's pledges. These are contained in the sunuds given to each taluqdar. By these documents the full proprietary right in the villages composing the taluquas was granted on condition that "all holding under them should be secured in the possession of all the subordinate rights they formerly enjoyed." His Excellency was aware that the rights principally in view were those of the maliks or village proprietors; but His Excellency was also fully convinced both that there was no intention on the part of the Government to abandon the rights of cultivators, if such existed, to the mercy of the taluqdar, and also that the wording of the sunud was so cautiously and widely framed as to prevent any such intention being fairly deduced from its terms.

It appeared to the Governor-General that whilst, on the one hand, there was no bar, either in good faith or law, to the recognition and registration of whatever rights of cultivators could be proved to exist, and, on the other, that no sufficient inquiry had been made concerning the fact of their existence, it was simply a duty incumbent on the Government, and in perfect harmony with the intention which had heretofore been expressed, to make provision for the impartial hearing of all such claims.

Appointment of Sir Henry Davies to conduct the Investigation.

An inquiry was accordingly ordered to be instituted into the alleged occupancy rights of cultivators; the appointment of a

Financial Commissioner was revived, and Mr. R. H. Davies, who served as Secretary to the Punjab Government, was appointed to the office, and entrusted with the work of investigation.

The Chief Commissioner was peremptorily directed (October 1864) to request the Financial Commissioner to revise all the revenue circulars regarding the occupancy rights of cultivators. The statement that they have no right of occupancy at fixed rents may be true in fact; but any claim to hold at fixed rates should be investigated and decided on its merits. It was added that it remained to be proved that there were no rights of beneficial occupancy; and that all claims to hold at low rates should be investigated and decided on their merits in the same way as claims for under-proprietary rights.

The Viceroy's Manifesto—Book Circular, No. 2, 1864.

Mr. Davies, the new Financial Commissioner, lost no time in entering upon his invidious duties. He received orders at once to make a 'careful' investigation into the rights of cultivators other than tenants-at-will, and if judicially proved to exist, to register them in the settlement records. On the 24th of October 1864, he issued his famous Book Circular No. 2 to all Commissioners: "It is not now admissible," he says, "to raise the question whether rights of occupancy at rates below the maximum rent are in an economical sense advantageous or the contrary. The simple point for determination is, whether, according to the usage of the country, such rights are recognized and enjoyed or not? If such rights are proved to exist, they must, like other landed tenures, be maintained, whatever opinion be held concerning their tendency.

"It has been stated that, in Oudh, no rights of occupancy of any kind exist, and that all non-proprietary cultivators are of one description,—namely, tenants at the will of the landowner. It remains, however, to be proved whether this statement is correct, or whether similar rights of occupancy to those recorded at the settlement of the North-West Provinces are possessed by cultivators in any or all of the districts of Oudh.

"The Government of India is of opinion that, in consequence of exclusion of claims of cultivators from hearing during the progress of the settlement, sufficient opportunity has not been given for the investigation, or sufficient data accumulated for the decision of the question as to whether these customary rights exist or not; and has directed that an impartial hearing shall be given to all claims preferred to them, and that whatever rights on the part of non-proprietary cultivators can be proved to exist shall be recognized and recorded.

"It will be necessary to make an investigation in every village to determine what cultivators, if any, have a right of occupancy either at fixed, or beneficial, or market-rates. It is advisable that this should be commenced simultaneously in each district under settlement."

Alarm of the Taluqdars.

Now the taluqdars were thoroughly alarmed, and there was a panic throughout the province. People thought that the events of 1856 were going to be repeated again, that the taluqdars were going to be deprived of their proprietary rights in favor of their tenants.

Opinions of the Press.

The *Oudh Gazette.*

It was pointed out by the *Oudh Gazette*, the organ of the taluqdars, that the opening of such a question would lead to most mischievous results; it would shake the confidence of the landholders in the pledged faith of Government, sow dissension between them and their tenants, open the door to interminable litigation, and create false hopes in the cultivators, and thus wasting the energies and resources of the people, impede the progress of the country. There would be an universal panic, and the value of property would be considerably depreciated.

It was remarked that the Government of India proposed to create a new right in this province—a right which had produced such baneful consequences in the North-West. Its purport was to strip the taluqdars of proprietary rights which they had enjoyed from time immemorial, to wrench from them what was their own, and which had been guaranteed to them by Her Majesty's representative in open Durbar, and in solemnly executed sunuds. But as this could not be accomplished openly in the face of equity, the method employed was to set at nought the experience of the Chief Commissioner and other veteran Settlement Officers upon the assumption that the inquiries hitherto made were conducted in a negligent and perfunctory manner. Fresh investigation was instituted to prove that these alleged rights were customary!

In some villages appertaining to taluqdars the rate of assessment was stationary for years, and the holdings were held by the same families of peasants; in some the assessment varied, and the holdings changed hands. This varied state of things was attributable to the character and disposition of their landlords and tenants. There were of course innumerable cases where the same family possessed holdings for generations, and often at the same rent. But none of these cases furnish a proof of the alleged right of occupancy, for the universal practice of exchanging pattas and kabuliyats (leases) which obtains in Oudh falsifies such an idea. In rare cases, where beneficial occupancy exists, the right was registered and acknowledged both by the Government and the taluqdars. In further denial of the occupancy rights, a peculiar annual ceremony between the landlord and his tenants may be noticed. The right possessed by the tenant in the holding he had for the past year ceases by the expiration of his patta, and a new engagement is entered upon for the ensuing year; add to this, the landlord or his agent is obliged to go and see the ceremony of manuring the land, as an earnest of his recognition of the right he grants by patta to the tenant to cultivate the land for the year. The ceremony mentioned above is, that, at the expiration of the year, when application is made for a fresh patta, the landlord or his agent goes to the village, and there the tenants gather round him, when he touches with his hand the basket containing manure, and directs them to manure the fields for which he intends granting a patta, and pronounces a blessing upon the work and receives a nuzzur of one or two rupees in acknowledgment of his absolute right of property. He afterwards grants the patta to those who manure the fields, and give the kabuliyats to him. Had there been any right of occupancy, why this ceremony, and why this universal and immemorial practice of exchanging pattas and kabuliyats? The ryot knew very well that the time for which the patta was granted having expired, the right he had in the holding had lapsed to the landholder who had given it. He did not, therefore, feel himself entitled to manure the field he held the previous year without the landlord's public and solemn permission to do so.

Of what use, it was pertinently asked, was the gift of "heritable transferable proprietary right" in the sunuds, if the taluqdars could not do with their land as they liked? They could not surely be called 'proprietors,' if others claimed beneficial occupancy on their estates. "The right of property," says Blackstone, "consists in a man's free use, enjoyment, and disposal of the land he owns. The proprietor is the absolute master of his estates; and he exercises a sole and despotic dominion over his property, to the total exclusion of all other individuals in the universe." The gift of proprietary right, it was indignantly urged, unaccompanied by all its privileges, was a simple mockery and delusion. The tendency of the Governor-General's high-handed measures in Oudh, it was said, was nothing more nor less than the reversal of Lord Canning's policy in Oudh.

The note of alarm thus sounded by the *Oudh Gazette* was taken up by the Press of India and England.

The *Englishman.*

"To stir up discord and litigation," said the *Englishman*, "to encourage falsehood and chicanery, by persuading people that they are the victims of oppression of which they are unconscious, has long been the most characteristic error of our policy in India. To have let well alone, and to have suffered a contented people to remain contented, would have deprived us of the morbid pleasure we seem to derive from becoming the champions of the oppressed. Armed with glasses far from achromatic, and possessing at the same time high magnifying powers, we have been almost uniformly successful in our quixotic search after grievances. Not long ago a whole province was disturbed by a proclamation to all discontents to come forward and complain of their wrongs.

We have scarcely recovered from the effects of this mischievous interference, when we are astounded by a much more important proclamation of a similar nature, yet more uncalled for, and calculated to provoke more disastrous results. We can regard the late proceedings of the Viceroy with reference to the settlement in Oudh, as nothing less than a proclamation inviting a people *en masse* to come forward and initiate an agrarian revolution.

"Were the measure of the Viceroy confined to the protection of rights already claimed and found to exist, it might be questionable whether any considerations of economy should be allowed to interfere with it. At the same time, in determining whether the Government should endeavour to discover rights neither claimed nor known to exist, it would be by no means irrelevant to consider first, whether it would be conducive to the welfare of the country that those rights should be put forward and sustained. The tendency of this measure must be to convert the taluqdars into mere tehsildars without interest in the estates which will be theirs only in name.

"We consider the measure of the Viceroy vicious, also because it is politically dangerous. It strikes at the very root of the dearest interest of one of the most warlike and powerful bodies of landed gentry in India. It is but a short time since these men were our implacable enemies; and it was the very policy which this measure seeks to overturn that contributed more than anything else to their conciliation. Not only is this measure inconsistent with that policy, but from its never having been sought by the ryot himself, it is of a nature to excite in the taluqdars of Oudh the feeling that it is not for the sake of the ryots, but out of ill-will to them that the Government is about to ruin them."

The *Press.*

Public opinion in England was aroused, and it spoke with no uncertain voice. The *Press*, one of the most powerful organs of the Conservative Party, in a series of articles condemned in severe terms the measures of Sir John Lawrence in Oudh. Other English papers took up the question, and Parliament directed its attention to the subject.

"It seems," said the *Press*, in speaking of the sunuds, that "the rights thus solemnly guaranteed Sir John Lawrence is now desirous of infringing, provided the Home Government are unwise and unfaithful enough to allow the Governor-General to carry out a crotchet of the Thomasonian school, and thereby take the most effectual means of subverting the independence of the taluqdars as landlords, and destroying the ancient system under which they inherited their lands from their ancestors. The Viceroy in fact is desirous of stepping in between the taluqdar and his tenants, and prescribing to him the rate at which he must let his lands; he would take from the taluqdar the right which he has always possessed of making his own bargains with his ryots and with the cultivators or large farmers upon his estates; and he would introduce into Oudh the practice which has not only ignominiously broken down, but which brought about the most iniquitous and disastrous results in the North-Western Provinces of India.

"The proposal of Sir John Lawrence to interfere between the taluqdars of Oudh and their tenants, and to prescribe to them the rate of rent which they should demand from the cultivators of the soil, or from those who farm their lands, is nothing more nor less than a direct infraction of the proprietary rights which the taluqdars have either inherited from their ancestors, or else have obtained by purchase,—rights which were solemnly guaranteed to them by our Government only six years ago.

"If this proposal of Sir John Lawrence be sanctioned, it will effectually undo all the beneficial work which, thanks to Lord Stanley, was accomplished in Oudh under the administration of Lord Canning. The great principles that were enumerated in Her Majesty's most gracious Proclamation to the princes, chiefs, and people of India,—the engagements which that document contained,—and the solemn promises which were made to the taluqdars of Oudh in person by Lord Canning—promises which were subsequently ratified by Lord Elgin—will be set at nought. We shall break faith, as faith was never broken before, with the people of India; and only six years after Her Majesty's Proclamation throughout the country as the Empress of Hindustan, we shall again proclaim by our actions that promises to which the sanction of royalty was given (and we even called the Almighty to witness, that they should be sacredly kept) have no binding power whatever on our consciences.

"Can we as a nation disregard in this manner the plainest rights, the most sacred promises, and act thus dishonorably and shamefully? We cannot believe it, for if we do so, not only will the promising fruit of the last six years be destroyed, but our good name for truth and honesty, which has always been our pillar of strength in India, will be for ever tarnished."

The Taluqdars' Meeting.

The taluqdars assembled at Lucknow on the 20th of December 1864 to take into consideration the constitutional means that should be adopted to protect taluqdari rights. The Maharaja of Bulrampore, the respected head of the taluqdars, assured the assembled chiefs, that so long as the taluqdars would treat their ryots as they ought to do, the Government would always cheerfully protect the just rights and privileges of the landowners of the province; and as he believed that there was none among his brethren who did otherwise, the Government, he had no doubt, would be kind to them, and would on no account infiringe the terms of the sunuds granted to them.

The late Maharaja Mansing, who was then the Vice-President of the British Indian Association of Oudh, made a most thoughtful speech. "The British Government," he said, "mercifully, justly, and wisely restored our estates to us on several conditions: One of these was, that all holding under us 'should be secured in the possession of all the subordinate rights they *formerly* enjoyed.' You recollect that many disputes arose regarding the meaning of these words. It has been finally decided, however, not that we should acknowledge and protect any newly-created rights, but that we are bound to maintain the rights which were in existence under us before the Annexation. I am sure there is no one in this assembly who does not understand the condition as it has been interpreted. The rights of those who possessed them on our estates before we became British subjects are to be preserved. How we have dealt with these, the history of the past six years shows. Where the rights were really in existence, they have been acknowledged by us.

"Now the question is, do the cultivators on our lands possess occupancy rights? If they possessed these rights before Oudh came under British rule, no one will be allowed to evict them from their holdings as long as they pay their equitable dues. If these rights belong to our tenants, we cannot overbear them. I do not suppose there is any one among us who would deny this, and would wish to take away the property of those who have eaten our salt for ages. Religion, morality, law and social usages would all combine to compel us to give up what is not our own. But we submit that the alleged rights into which the Financial Commissioner institutes an enquiry did not exist in Oudh before the British rule was established in the province. We were absolute proprietors of our own. We could dispose of our property in any way we liked, and no power in the land could restrain us from doing so.

"The sunuds gave us proprietary rights in our estates. But what are these proprietary rights without the power of disposing of our own? They are practically of no value without it—a shadow without substance.

"Let people say what they like, I, for my own part, believe that the Sovereign who has been so kind to us, who rescued us from perils unnumbered, will not take away our proprietary rights so solemnly given. We ought to assure Her Majesty and Her Viceroy that we cannot oppress our ryots, that we look upon them as members of our own family, and that our mutual interest is our best security against anything like oppression. I assure you, brethren, that if, from any error, our Government has opened an inquiry that will create false hopes in our ryots, and subject them to deceptions in all shapes and forms, so soon as our rulers perceive their mistake, they will be the first to repair our wrongs, and confirm the rights and privileges which they themselves guaranteed. We may have some trouble to properly represent our grievances; but as soon as this is done, the English nation will cheerfully restore our just rights to us. I have been told that the English people respect their laws very much. These rights have been secured to us by the laws of

England, and those laws will maintain them. You need not despair, you have nothing to fear."

The speeches of the taluqdars excited considerable discussion both in England and India, and the sensation they created was so great that the country demanded with one voice that justice should be done to the taluqdars. The leading Indian newspaper (*Englishman*) thus spoke of them:—

"The taluqdars of Oudh speak out like men for the rights which the Viceroy has had the impolicy to attack. Their case could scarcely have been put more forcibly than they have put it themselves; yet the most critical of judges could discover no violation of good taste, and the most despotic of censors no disregard of the respect due to authority, in what they have said. They spoke like brave men, who know that brave men are not to be scared from their purpose by words, and like men of sound good sense, who know that what they have to say will command more attention said moderately than insolently or defiantly. As to the matter of what was said at the meeting, no morally and actually just man—no conscientious man who is not prejudiced, will deny that the taluqdars deprecate a grievous wrong; and at the same time, no man of science, no political economist, will deny that they deprecated a formidable calamity—a calamity not only to themselves, but to their country."

The Tenant-Right Question in Parliament.

Public men in England looked with suspicion upon the proceedings of the Viceroy in Oudh. There was an almost unanimous opinion that Sir John Lawrence was trying to reverse Lord Canning's Revenue System in Oudh. The inquiry ordered to be instituted by him was considered as only the thin end of the wedge. The Viceroy was determined, it was thought, to assimilate the land tenures of Oudh with those existing in the Punjab and the North-Western Provinces. The policy of the Viceroy was condemned as highly impolitic and dangerous to the peace and prosperity of India; while at the same time the breach of faith that it would involve would be derogatory to the character of Great Britain. While public feeling was wound up to the highest pitch, Lord Stanley took the question in hand,

and asked the Secretary of State, in the House of Commons, whether the inquiry then being carried on into the respective rights of the taluqdars and the cultivators of Oudh was in pursuance of instructions issued by him, and whether he would lay upon the table any correspondence that might have passed on the subject; and also whether he could give any explanation of the nature and purport of the inquiry.

The Secretary of State (Sir Charles Wood) said, in reply, that the great feature of Lord Canning's policy with regard to the settlement of Oudh was to restore the taluqdars to the position of independent native landowners and gentlemen, and to make the settlement direct with them in lieu of the system which had prevailed in the North-West Provinces of a settlement with the under-proprietors. "That remains perfect and altogether untouched;" but there was a question as to the existence of certain rights of cultivators in Oudh. The Chief Commissioner admitted frankly that if they did exist they were preserved under the sunuds of Lord Canning to the taluqdars, in which a condition was inserted that all the rights of persons holding under them and subordinate to them should be secured: and the object of the inquiry ordered by Sir John Lawrence was simply to ascertain whether these rights did or did not exist. If the result should be that they did not exist, there was an end of the question. If the result should be that they did exist, then it would be the duty of Government, under the stipulations of Lord Canning's grant to the taluqdars, to respect them. It was not in consequence of any instructions from home that the inquiry was ordered.

This was the statement which was given by the Secretary of State in explanation of the Viceroy's policy in Oudh, but he knew very well that the English people would not be satisfied with his mere *ipse dexit,* but would want substantial proofs of the sincerity of the declarations made by the Government. The question was, whether the Government was justified at all in instituting an inquiry which might lead to a reversal of the policy of Lord Canning in Oudh, and which, under the colour of protecting subordinate rights, would result in a breach of faith with the taluqdars of Oudh. The word of the British Sovereign once pledged was pledged for ever, and that which was done in the name of the British nation must be upheld. The question of expediency was not to be taken into consideration at all. "Be assured," said Lord Canning to the taluqdars in open Durbar (October 26, 1859), "that as long as each of you is a loyal and faithful subject, his rights and dignity as a taluqdar will be upheld by me and every representative of our Queen, and that no man shall disturb them." In spite of these solemn pledges given by Lord Canning, here was a new Viceroy who, it was said, was trying to destroy taluqdari rights, and introduce the communistic system of the North-West into Oudh. The provisions of the sunuds which Sir John Lawrence twisted into a charter of occupancy rights, could never be construed as including the question of such alleged rights. They simply referred to under-proprietary rights, and not to the cultivating rights of the ryots. Lord Canning gave absolute proprietary rights to the taluqdars. By what authority then it was asked could the Governor-General create a new body of proprietors in the estate of which the taluqdars were proprietors ?

Sir Charles Wood's Despatch.

The explanation by Sir Charles Wood on behalf of Sir John Lawrence was made in the House of Commons on the 10th of February 1865. On the same day he sent a Despatch to the Viceroy embodying his views on the serious questions which were then so warmly discussed. "He (Mr. Wingfield) says," writes Sir Charles Wood, "that the sunuds which the taluqdars hold only provide for the maintenance of rights previously enjoyed; and they might fairly urge that it would be a violation of the guarantee if new rights be created to their prejudice. I do not understand that any one proposes this, or contends for more than the preservation of rights which formerly existed. It seems to me that, under any circumstances, the only point to be determined is the single question of fact, whether any occupancy rights on the part of cultivating ryots did or did not exist at the time of Annexation. If such rights existed, and were unaffected by the orders of the Government of India, they exist now as they existed then. If they existed and were affected by the orders of the Government, they were restored and secured by the sunuds. In either case, the only foundation on which they can rest is their previous existence at the time of Annexation.

"It is of the greatest importance to reassure the taluqdars, and to remove any impression that there is a wish to create new rights, or resuscitate rights which had become obsolete, or to adopt any measure to their disadvantage, *now or hereafter*, which can militate against their superior position, or affect the subordinate character of all holding rights in their taluquas.

"It is not to be forgotten that the great object of Lord Canning's policy in the settlement of Oudh was to maintain in that province a class of superior native landholders in an influential position, and whom he invested also with considerable administrative and judicial powers. This policy had the full approval of the Home Government.

"Every report which had been received from the province speaks in terms of high commendation, not only of the loyalty which the taluqdars have displayed in various ways, but of the highly creditable manner in which they have exercised the powers entrusted to them."

It would be matter of deep regret, added Sir Charles Wood, if, in carrying the recent measures into execution, any reasonable cause of complaint was given to the taluqdars. He was extremely anxious that the measures ordered by the Government of India should not be pushed beyond what was indispensably requisite for this purpose, and that every consideration should be shown to the taluqdars, so as not in any way to lower their position in the eyes of the country. After what had taken place in Oudh, and the expectations which the taluqdars had been led to entertain as to the effect of Lord Canning's measure, "I am confident," he continued, "that you will see the propriety of taking especial care, without sacrificing the just rights of others, to maintain the taluqdars of Oudh in that position of consideration and dignity which Lord Canning's Government contemplated conferring upon them."

The taluqdars of Oudh have never wished to sacrifice "the just rights of others." All that they wish is that their own rights, guaranteed to them by their Sovereign, should be secured to them in such a manner that no Viceroy may ever be able to disturb them. They have faithfully observed the conditions of the sunuds, and they expect that the British Government should respect the promises which were made to them. An inexperienced officer brings groundless charges against them as bad landlords, and a cry is raised at once that another body of proprietors should be created in their own estates, and the taluqdars should be converted into mere tax-gatherers. Nothing could be further from their wish, as we said, than to disturb the just rights of others, but they anxiously wish that no *new rights* should be created in their estates, and that no measures should be adopted which would militate against their superior position. Their case can scarcely be put more forcibly than the Secretary of State had put it for them.

Dissent of Members of the Indian Council.

Sir James Hogg.

Sir James Hogg, of the Council of the Secretary of State for India, dissented from this Despatch. "The sunuds were granted," he says, "for political reasons, and in construing them, we must look to what Lord Canning intended to grant and what the taluqdars believed they had received, and not to seek to restrict the rights and privileges of the taluqdars by discussing the terms, as if we were arguing an English conveyance. In the correspondence and discussions previous to issuing the sunuds, no right is mentioned or alluded to, except proprietary rights; and I think it was clearly the intention of Lord Canning to restore the native aristocracy to their ancient position and dignity, and to give the taluqdars the entire dominion over their estates, subject only to sub-proprietary rights. After granting the sunuds, instructions were issued by the Chief Commissioner in accordance with the meaning and intention of Lord Canning. They directed that proprietary rights only should be recorded, and expressly excluded occupancy rights. These instructions were approved by Lord Canning, who granted the sunuds, and also by Lord Elgin, and have been acted upon for five years. It is alleged that the approval of the instructions was general, as if the special point of occupancy rights might have escaped notice; but Mr. Grey says, 'nor can it be supposed that the point was overlooked by the then Governor-General, for it was specifically adverted to, and approved in the 8th paragraph of the reply to the Chief Commissioner.'

"So clear and specific were the instructions issued by the Chief Commissioner, and the approval of them by Government, that it was suggested that, under the provisions of the (India) Council's Act, they had the force of law. This point was considered so doubtful that a case on the subject was submitted to the Advocate-General, who was of opinion that the proceedings had not the force of law. *I cannot, however, admit that public faith is less binding than legal obligation.* There never was even a suggestion as to the existence of any occupancy rights till three years after the sunuds were granted, when the Judicial Commissioner in his report stated that such rights did exist. But conceding that there had been some rights of occupancy, and that under the condition in the sunuds it might be argued that they are preserved, I contend that the question is not now open. It has been decided by competent authority, and that decision has been ratified by two Governments and acted upon for five years; and in my opinion it cannot be departed from without a violation of public faith that could not fail to create distrust, not only throughout Oudh, but throughout India. I fear that other grants and concessions made by Lord Canning, after quelling the Mutiny, including the right of adoption, may be regarded as having been made under the pressure of the times, and that they may be withdrawn by some future Government. But why, I ask, has this question been raised? Was there any practical grievance to redress? Has it been alleged that the taluqdars have been cruel, unjust, or oppressive to their ryots? Have the ryots been crying for justice, or claiming for rights withheld? On the contrary, the province is tranquil and prosperous, the taluqdars are reported as kind landlords, loyal subjects acting up to the wishes of Government, and aiding their views, and the people contented and happy.

"Why disturb this tranquillity and contentment by attempting to obtrude on the province a right resisted by the taluqdars, and not asked for by the ryots, and, as it appears to me, only to vindicate a very questionable theory ?"

Sir Erskine Perry.

"On reading over the whole of the papers," said Sir Erskine Perry, "I come to the conclusion that Mr. Wingfield's decision was quite right; but even if it were not, I cannot agree with Sir John Lawrence that sound policy requires these occupancy rights to be resuscitated.

"I should greatly prefer to see the relations which have existed between taluqdars and ryots going on as they have done for centuries, governed by mutual convenience, mutual interests, and the usages of native society, than to see stringent laws introduced, founded on English notions, of landlord and tenant, for the history of British India is full of examples of the great mischief done by clothing imperfect theories in the rigid form of law."

Mr. Macnaghten.

"In the sunuds," said Mr. Macnaghten, "Lord Canning intended to protect, and did sufficiently protect, the interests of 'sub-proprietors,' and of 'all persons holding an interest in the land under the taluqdars,' and he intended to confer, and did actually confer, by such sunuds, on the taluqdars, all and every other right and property in their respective taluquas; and the taluqdars of Oudh, in their communicatons with the Chief Commissioner, were led to believe that no occupancy rights were recognized by the British Government. Those who maintain that 'occupancy rights' have existed in Oudh, admit that such rights are indefinite and undefinable. In my opinion, it is the worst possible policy to disturb the relations which, during the last four or five years, have subsisted between the taluqdar and the ryot; no grounds whatever, either of complaint by the ryot, or injustice or wrong done by the taluqdar, having been adduced in justification of the proceeding."

CHAPTER IV.

CONCLUSION OF THE INVESTIGATION.

In the meantime the local investigations which were fully and fairly made, in knots of twenty-five villages in each district, under Mr. Davies's Circular, only proved how very right the taluqdars had been in their denial of occupancy rights, and how very wrong was the Viceroy, who, acting on a foregone conclusion, had directed the inquiry. The measures of the Viceroy caused, not unnaturally, apprehension in the minds of the taluqdars, who have had ample reason to believe, from the instructions issued by Lord Canning and Sir Charles Wingfield, that their proprietary rights would never be touched, and that the so-called occupancy rights would never be created in their estates. The inquiry proved without the shadow of a doubt that, in an infinitesimally small number of cases, which from their very nature were exceptional, such alleged rights were a myth in Oudh. "Nothing could be more complete than the triumph of the truth. Power and prejudice had done their worst. Might had for a time triumphed over right, but at last the case became too plain for denial." Create them he might, if the Viceroy dared to set at nought the pledged faith of the British Sovereign; but hereditary tenants with beneficial occupancy—"those revenue nightmares, which press so heavily in the North-Western Provinces on the still sleeping genius of agricultural progress," did not and, thanks to Lord Canning, Sir Charles Wingfield, and his worthy successors, do not exist in Oudh.

Results.

We will, in Mr. Davies's own words, state the result of the judicial investigation as to the existence of the rights of cultivation and occupancy ordered by the Government of India. "With the exception of the Settlement Officer of Hurdui (Mr. Bradford)," says Mr. Davies, "all are agreed that no right of hereditary occupancy was recognized in the ryot under the native Government. I have examined the cases investigated by Mr. Bradford, and find that in none does any cultivator assert a right to remain in the land in opposition to the will of the zemindar.

Sir Henry Davies's Report.

"It is necessary to explain that one important class of ryots, namely, the descendants of former village zemindars, still retaining some beneficial interest in the holdings, are protected by the Oudh rules. As regards the existence of a right of occupancy, otherwise derived than from former proprietorship, I conceive that the reports of the Settlement Officers leave no room for doubt; and that it is proved that, previous to Annexation, no such right was asserted by a cultivator against his zemindar.

"That, during the recent enquiries, the members of this class (high caste cultivators of the Brahmin and Rajpoot class), bold and comparatively intelligent as they must be admitted to be, and practically enjoying, as they generally do, a beneficial interest in the soil, should, as a body, have abstained from asserting any right of occupancy, is certainly strong evidence that they had no recognized rights under the native Government.

"It must, I apprehend, be inferred that the registration of the possession of a right of occupancy by the ryots of twelve or more years' standing in the North-Western Provinces, was rather in pursuance of a deliberate policy, aiming at the preservation of fixity of occupancy founded on the expediency of moderating rents, and justifiable by the increased value given to land by the fiscal measures of Government than in recognition of claims judicially made good by the ryots themselves. There is, however, a difference in the circumstances of Oudh.

"The Financial Commissioner, therefore, came to the conclusion that the evidence completely went to show that no length of occupancy maintained by a ryot under the native Government gave him a right to hold his land against the will of his zemindars; that, according to custom, the zemindars rarely ejected cultivators who held their fields in common, so long as they paid the rent demanded; that when rent was enhanced by the zemindars, it was generally raised in proportion to the capacity of the land, and in accordance with the amount paid for similar land in the neighbourhood, and that most frequently the rents of all the cultivators in the same village were raised at the same time; and that competition was almost unknown."

"The cultivators," Mr. Davies went on to say, "have had the fullest opportunity, in all the districts in which the enquiry has been made, of stating their claims. Their depositions have been taken down by the Settlement Officers themselves, and no trouble has been spared to induce them to speak out. I myself have also frequently, when alone, questioned them at their fields and at their wells, but always with the same result."

Here was a complete triumph for the taluqdars of Oudh. Most full and unquestionable evidence was obtained that no occupancy rights existed in Oudh. Sir Charles Wingfield, on receiving Mr. Davies's Report, informed the Governor-General (July 14, 1865) that the investigation had been most fully and fairly made, and that no trace of occupancy right could be found in Oudh. "The Secretary of State," wrote Sir Charles Wingfield, "in his Despatch (February 10, 1865), has defined the question for decision to be 'whether any occupancy rights on the part of cultivating ryots did or did not exist at the time of Annexation. The only foundation on which they can rest is their existence at the time of Annexation.' This question appears to the Chief Commissioner to be answered in the negative by the Financial Commissioner."

Sir Charles Wingfield's remarks.

As regards the first conclusion of Mr. Davies, Sir Charles Wingfield entirely concurred. Indeed it is worthy of notice that the few cultivators, who had come forward to claim occupancy rights, gave as their sole reason that the British rule conferred such rights, and owned that they had not had them under the native Government.

The Chief Commissioner admitted that it was the custom seldom to evict cultivators. This custom was dictated by self-interest and common sense, as well as good feeling. Why, indeed, should landholders seek to get rid of tenants who would pay the full rent for which the land could be let? In Oudh there was so much waste land that the cultivators would always be welcomed on another estate. No landlord, therefore, would wish to get rid of his ryots. He was perhaps more dependent on them than they on him.

With regard to the conclusion that the enhancement of rent was in proportion to the capabilities of the soil, there could be no second opinion as to the reasonableness of the custom by which the rents were raised. It would be useless for the landlord to demand a higher rent than the capabilities of the land, *i.e.*, its productive powers, would warrant, for no one would give it. This is no more than saying that the land lets for what it is supposed to be worth, and what can be obtained for it. The right of the taluqdar to demand what rent he pleased for his land is proved to have existed; but, in common with the owner of every other kind of property, he was obliged to limit his demand to what he could get for it.

It is the general practice for the landlord to give the cultivator in occupation, provided he has no cause for being dissatisfied with him, the refusal at the enhanced rates demanded, or offered by others; because the landlord can have no wish to turn out an old tenant who would pay him as much as he could get from any one else. The landlord's right to do what he pleased with his land cannot be said to be limited by reason of his not having exercised it in a senseless way, and to his own injury. The preference given to an old tenant at the rent demanded is no more than the consideration that any tradesman would, if he had the opportunity, show to an old customer.

With reference to the statement that competition was almost unknown, it may be remarked that although there may not be general competition throughout a district, there is local competition, and competition within the village. The large rents paid by the gardening classes for land near cities and large villages, and the fact that the inlying lands of a village let for higher rents than the more distant, indicate that there is rivalry for them. We see new cultivators constantly settled in villages, and many of these men must have been forced by competition to quit their native villages.

Sir Charles Wingfield feared that the Financial Commissioner, after having first proved that there were no rights of occupancy in Oudh, and thus decided the issue fixed by the Secretary of State, next endeavoured to show that custom had created something like them with a view of opening a way for legislative interference at some future time. "A fair use," he says, "is not made of the word 'custom,' when the most natural action, the motives for which must exist in every age and in all relations of life, is set down to custom, if by it is meant a usage having the force of authority. A custom that one of the parties can disregard at pleasure, that cannot be enforced by an appeal to authorities, or to public opinion, cannot have prescriptive force. The only custom the Chief Commissioner can discover from these reports, as regulating the relations of landlord and tenant, was the will of the former restrained in its exercise by a sense of his own interests, and his dependence on the cultivators of the soil, of which the latter were perfectly well aware. The relation was not a custom having a tendency to become a right on the part of the tenant, but a bond of mutual dependence which must long continue to subsist between the parties."

Origin of the Taluqdars.

There is one passage in the Chief Commissioner's letter, which is well worthy of notice. He clearly exposes the ignorance of those who are unacquainted with the true character and history of the Oudh taluqdars. Mr. Thomason's definition of a taluqdar, as a middleman put in to collect the revenue, does not at all apply to the class in Oudh. "In Government letter of 30th September 1864," says Sir Charles Wingfield, "it was stated that the taluqdari tenure of Oudh is identical with the zemindari of Bengal. If this means that the taluqdars generally were of the same class and origin as the zemindars with whom the Permanent Settlement was made, according to the generally received account of the latter, which represents them as farmers-general, or revenue agents of the Mahomedan Government, having no proprietary connection with the land (though the Chief Commissioner entertains some doubt of the correctness of the description), the Chief Commissioner would beg to be allowed to correct this supposition. The great majority of the Hindu taluqdars of Oudh are heads of houses, whose ancestors acquired their possessions by colonization and conquest between the years 1200 and 1300 A.D. The first settlers were fugitives from the Mahomedan invasion of Upper India, and from them descend all the great families in Eastern Oudh. (Two great tribes of Rajpoots, Bisens and Baises, are said to have settled prior to the 13th Century, under the protection of the Rathore dynasty of Kanouj, to whom all Oudh was nominally subject.) The later settlers formed with their followers part of Mahomedan armies sent to reduce the province. Oudh was then half-waste, and inhabited by Bhurs, Arruks, and Taroos, who are believed by European writers to have been aboriginal races. These were subjugated so effectually that no trace of the two former is to be found, except amongst the very lowest classes of the population. The Taroos have retired into the forests underneath and within the hills. No independent proprietorship, therefore, can now be traced prior to the Rajpoot occupation.

"Each clan was under a head, in whom all authority and proprietorship were vested; but the clans became divided into houses, the heads of which are the present taluqdars. There was much subdivision among the younger branches, and village communities were thus formed; but the rule of the Guddee or Primogeniture, which subsequently grew up, was a check on further subdivision, and eventually the descendants of the younger branches and the village communities were by force or consent reunited under the head of the house, who also increased his possessions by the incorporation of villages held by other castes and held by Rajpoots of other tribes. Sometimes the subdivision went on until the clans broke up entirely into village communities, as in the Unao and Lucknow Districts, in which there are few or no taluqdars left. It will thus be seen that, among Rajpoots, the taluqdari tenure, or proprietorship of a single head, is older than the village tenure.

"This description, the Chief Commissioner believes, is generally applicable to nearly all the Rajpoot taluqdars, who form by far the larger portion of the class. Some few of the Mahomedan taluqdars are Rajpoot converts, and in everything but religion retain their Hindu customs.

"The ancestors of some of the Mahomedan taluqdars were officers in the Royal armies, who received grants of land on the conquest of the country. Some, however, came from the provinces under the Jouanpore dynasty, which ceased to reign about the middle of the 16th Century. The Chief Commissioner knows of three bankers or capitalists only, in Oudh, who have become taluqdars. Several taluqdars have acquired position and estates as Government officials, such as Nazims and Chukladars. But they are comparatively few in number. The Chief Commissioner cannot, at this moment, recollect above twenty who owe their possession to official position or Court favour. Indeed it is remarkable how little desirous Court favorites seem to have been to get land."

The Tenant-Right Question in the House of Lords.

While the Financial Commissioner and the Chief Commissioner were busy in writing reports giving the results of the investigation which had unsettled the minds of the landowners of Oudh for the last ten months, the Marquis of Clanricarde asked the Under-Secretary of State, in the House of Lords, whether the Governor-General of India had taken steps to inquire into titles to land in other parts of India similar to those which were adopted in the Province of Oudh. He believed that, above all things, it was desirable, in legislating for India, to lay down no particular rule for the government of the whole country, but that, in the regulation of each portion, regard should be had to the usages, customs, and laws already existing. It should also be remembered that the taluqdars were men of wealth and position.

Lord Dufferin said, that when "any newly-acquired territory passed under the jurisdiction of the Indian Government, it was the practice of the Government immediately to despatch a staff of revenue officers and surveyors for the purpose of effecting what was technically known as the settlement of the property; in other words, to measure the various areas about to become subject to the land-tax, and to ascertain who were the persons responsible for the payment of that tax. That course was taken first for the purposes of fiscal assessment, and next, in order to record existing rights. The agricultural population of India was divided, as in Europe, into landlords and tenants. But the latter class was again subdivided into three classes—into (1) tenants-at-will; (2) tenants with rates of occupancy lower than the market-rate (that is to say, tenants who had a right from generation to generation at a fixed rate which was invariably lower than the market-rate); and (3) tenants who had a right of occupancy at what are called fair market-rates. The rights of the last class, though of considerable value, were not of the greatest importance, but those of the tenants at fixed rates were undoubtedly of a very valuable character. When this settlement of territory was effected, it was customary to record not only the rights of the proprietors, but also of those of the occupying tenants. This practice had been recognized as early as 1836 by Lord Auckland, and was subsequently confirmed by Lord Hardinge and other Governors-General. Lord Canning had also reserved the subsidiary rights of this class of occupiers, and consequently it was a mistake to imagine that the policy pursued by Sir John Lawrence was a reversal of that adopted by Lord Canning. It was in fact merely an extension and confirmation of that policy. When the time arrived for the final settlement of Oudh, and Mr. Wingfield reported to the Government upon the subject, it occurred to Sir John Lawrence to ask whether he had made any investigation as to the rights of occupancy. Though Mr. Wingfield felt perfectly satisfied from his knowledge of the country that no such rights existed, he said he had not instituted any investigation into the subject, and therefore thought it expedient to renew the inquiry. That inquiry had been conducted in the fairest and most impartial manner under the superintendence of Mr. Davies, a revenue officer, and the result was, that Mr. Wingfield's previous opinion had been to a great extent confirmed. Such was the result of that particular inquiry."

Lord Dufferin put the case before the House of Lords from Sir John Lawrence's point of view. The Viceroy instituted the inquiry in spite of Sir Charles Wingfield's repeated assurances that the subject was inquired into by him and other experienced Revenue Officers, who almost unanimously had come to the conclusion that no occupancy rights existed; that the taluqdars were the real proprietors, and their ryots were tenants-at-will. But let that pass The House was assured that the inquiry was conducted in the fairest and the fullest manner, and that no occupancy rights were found to exist in Oudh. His Lordship must have intended that as the inquiry was at an end, and no trace of occupancy was found in the province, the question must drop, and the taluqdars would remain, as before, absolute proprietors of their estates. The only foundation on which tenant-rights could be recognized was wanting, and there should, therefore, be no more discussion on the subject.

In forming this expectation, Lord Dufferin was somewhat precipitate. The question was not dropped till Parliament and the English people were fully satisfied that the Government had done full justice to the taluqdars, and that the rights guaranteed to them were perfectly unaffected and untouched by the unauthorized and unjustifiable measures of Sir John Lawrence.

The following extract from the report of the sitting of the House of Lords, on the 3rd of August 1866, will show that the interests of Oudh, which attracted so much notice during the last Session, were still borne in mind by those who had paid attention to the subject:—

"The Marquis of Clanricarde moved for copies of the report of the Financial Commissioner, Mr. Davies, upon the inquiry into the rights of occupancy in Oudh, together with the reports of the different Settlement Officers and Commissioners in Oudh, and of the evidence of the landowners, cultivators, and others upon the same subject; also for a copy of the despatch of the Chief Commissioner of Oudh forwarding the abovementioned reports to the Government of India, in February (July ?) 1865; and also for copy of the reply of the Governor-General of India to that despatch, and the further correspondence of the Chief Commissioner and the Governor-General on the subject up to the present time (August 3, 1866).

"The Earl of Malmsbury said there could be no objection to produce the two first returns, but the answer of the Governor-General and the observations made on the reports of the Commissioners had not reached this country. The Government had received a report of the Commissioners, the result of which, so far as the Government could judge, was that there was no such right as had been supposed by some persons in favor of the occupiers, and the cultivators themselves had almost unanimously given up all idea of any such right."

We see that the Governor-General had not communicated to the Secretary of State, so late as August 1866, his reply to the Chief Commissioner's despatch, forwarding the report of Sir Henry Davies. Many ill-natured remarks were naturally made on this circumstance. "Sir John Lawrence," it was said, "is determined, it seems, to keep the sore open; to irritate it under the guise of probing it; and thus keep it inflamed until such time as he can find an opportunity to treat it after his own fashion. The Viceroy's plan still seems to be to keep the Home Government imperfectly informed in order to prevent the case from being definitely settled by the Indian Minister. The Governor-General has proved himself to possess the happy knack of overlooking the most material points that tell against his views, while at the same time he professes to be wholly free from prejudice, and to be ardently bent on discovering and demonstrating the truth."

We must say this was not doing justice to the Viceroy. His motives were noble and benevolent, and the taluqdars always gave him credit for the feelings which actuated him. "The present Viceroy," said one of the speakers at the great meeting of the taluqdars on the 30th of December 1864, "has ordered the institution of this inquiry from motives than which none could be purer. His intentions are good. As soon as he shall be convinced that such a policy is ruinous both to the landlord and tenant, and that these rights never existed before, be assured that he himself would guarantee your rights in such a manner to you, that no other Governor-General after him would again open the question."

The speaker was quite right when he said that Sir John Lawrence was incapable of harbouring the motives which were ascribed to him. The policy he pursued was certainly benevolent, though mistaken, and to impugn his motives was anything but fair. The taluqdars did not for a moment dream that he would destroy their rights: they were fully aware that, as soon as he was convinced that the policy he was pursuing was injurious to the interests of the province, and that their rights were guaranteed in such a manner that the question of occupancy rights could never be opened again, he would desist from harassing them and take prompt measures to establish and confirm their rights on a surer and a firmer basis. "It has never been my intention," said Lord Lawrence (19th February 1866), "to interfere with the principles of his (Lord Canning's) policy, by which the general status of the taluqdars in that province was settled and defined after the Mutiny of 1857. In a word, I desired to adhere to the conditions of the grants given by Lord Canning, as I read and understood these documents, and as I believe they are reasonably to be read and understood, and according to their true intent and purport."

Lord Lawrence's disavowal of motives adverse to Lord Canning's policy.

His Excellency fully admitted that peace and prosperity were the general result of the present administration of Oudh. The expectations formed by the Oudh landlords were not disappointed by the Viceroy, and he was one of the foremost, as we shall presently show, of those who spoke in high terms of commendation of the conduct of the taluqdars during the inquiry and at the time of the subsequent arrangement, which gave satisfaction to all parties.

In reply to the Chief Commissioner's letter, dated 16th July 1865, the Governor-General informed Sir Charles Wingfield (February 16, 1866), that, in concurrence with him, he agreed generally in the result of the inquiry as summed up by Mr. Davies. "The evidence adduced," he says, "tends to show that, under the native Government of Oudh, there was vested in the ryot no right of occupancy which could be successfully maintained against the will of the landlord.

Non-existence of occupancy rights in Oudh fully established.

"Adverting to the relations formed and the expectations created by the present rules of law and procedure, to the general usage on which these rules are based, and to the evils that may be apprehended if that usage is entirely ignored by the Revenue Courts, His Excellency in Council is disposed to think that the most just and expedient course will be to maintain the present system as it stands.

"His Excellency in Council approves the suspension of the general inquiry into the rights of the ryots, and it need not be resumed."

In reply to this, Sir Charles Wingfield stated (March 1, 1866), that as the sunuds had conferred the full proprietary rights on the taluqdars, from which were excepted only subordinate rights held under them formerly, and as the Secretary of State had declared that no new rights would be created, and as the investigation recently held had conclusively established that no right of occupancy had existed at the time of Annexation, the conditions of the sunuds must be scrupulously maintained, and cultivating rights must on no account be created in the estates of the taluqdars. The whole argument of the Government letter, dated 30th September 1864, which directed the inquiry to be made, turned on the point, whether or not the rights in question existed when Lord Canning gave the sunuds to the taluqdars. If they did exist at the time, then it was no violation of the sunud to uphold them; but if they did not exist at that time, it was admitted, on all hands, they could not be created consistently with the terms of the sunuds. Sir Charles Wingfield reminded the Governor-General that when great apprehensions were created in the minds of the taluqdars by the recent measures of the Viceroy, he was directed to assure them that the *spirit* and *letter* of Lord Canning's policy and the conditions of his sunuds would be "scrupulously maintained;" and that he had issued a Circular to that effect. As Sir Henry Davies's inquiry with regard to the alleged rights had settled the question in the negative, the taluqdars were quite right in hoping that occupancy rights in no form whatever would be created in their estates.

The descendants of former proprietors.

Sir John Lawrence now desired to see some provision made for the protection of one class of tenants; he meant those ryots whose families had held the same lands for several generations, and were formerly possessed of some sort of proprietary right, though the present holders might have sunk to the position of mere occupying cultivators. Such ryots, Sir John thought, would not probably be found to comprise more than from 15 to 20 per cent. of the whole number of cultivators; and the taluqdars themselves, he believed, would hardly object to recognize the claim of such cultivators to more favorable terms than the mass of cultivators were entitled to.

CHAPTER V.

"THE COMPROMISE."

The taluqdars, when previously asked, had expressed their regret that they could not, consistently with the terms of the sunuds granted to them, agree to any sort of arrangement or compromise on the point of tenant-right. But that opinion was expressed with reference to the view then urged by the Governor-General that non-proprietary cultivators generally, who had held for a certain time, should be recorded as possessing a right of occupancy, and have their rents fixed for the term of settlement. Under the altered position of this point produced by Sir Henry Davies's Report, the taluqdars might be disposed, it was thought, to stand less stiffly on what they considered to be their full right than they were in 1864.

It was urged, on behalf of the taluqdars, that the issue of the recent inquiry as fixed by the Secretary of State, and accepted by the Government of India, was whether rights of occupancy existed at the Annexation; and, agreeably to the instructions of the Governor-General, the taluqdars were assured by the Chief Commissioner that this was the object and limit of the inquiry, and that if the result should be to prove that no such rights existed at Annexation, none would be created. This issue having been decided in the negative by the Financial Commissioner, it followed that all claims on behalf of the non-proprietary cultivators should be abandoned, and that no rights of occupancy of any kind should be acknowledged. The Secretary of State, it was added, had declared, in his Despatch of 10th February 1865, that their previous existence at the time of Annexation was the only foundation on which they could rest. But if it was still desired that some consideration should be shown to the descendants of former proprietors, or to such proprietors themselves who were then reduced to the condition of non-proprietary tillers of the soil, the taluqdars might agree to make a concession in their favor on the following clear and precise understanding:

That the taluqdars be assured that the Government renounces all intention to claim for other non-proprietary cultivators rights of occupancy arising from prescription, and not from special contract; and if the proposed arrangement in favor of the class referred to by the Governor-General be carried into effect, it be held to dispose finally of the tenant-question in Oudh.

The Governor-General said that he would be content not to press for the recognition of any rights of occupancy, or for any advantages to the cultivator which could not be individually proved to exist. The Viceroy was importuned that Mr. Davies's finding should be frankly accepted and fairly and fully acted upon, *except* with regard to the special class of cultivators in whose favor it was proposed that the taluqdars should concede a right of beneficial occupancy.

The following terms were now definitely proposed by Sir Charles Wingfield to the taluqdars:

On the one hand, taluqdars to grant favorable terms to all ex-proprietors or their descendants who had retained possession as cultivators of the fields they formerly occupied as proprietors in their ancestral villages, or estates, if their property consisted of more than one village. No distinction to be made between those who voluntarily parted with, or were forcibly dispossessed of, their proprietary rights.

On the other hand, no further measures would be taken by the Settlement Officers for enquiry into or record of any rights other than proprietary rights. But the Settlement Officers would hear and dispose of judicially any claims which cultivators might bring forward to any form of right, whether of mere occupancy at the rent the landlord chose to ask, or at beneficial rates.

The taluqdars submitted as follows:

" The terms which the Governor-General proposes to give us, end that we should give, seem inconsistent with our rights as they were before Annexation and as they are now secured by our sunuds.

"If we give low rents to ex-proprietors, such persons who have no rights by law or custom acquire thereby pretensions and ground of claims, for, in addition to other reasons, it is possible that hereafter some officers will hold that they (ex-proprietors) have kept their proprietary rights alive, as in the Morarkheira case (Ruling of F. C. that a lease, for however short a period, held by the former proprietors within the twelve years preceding Annexation, gives a right to the sub-settlement of the village), and may give them something more, although we give this of our free will; and there is this disadvantage in the offer made by the Governor-General, that the ancient rights which we had under the native Government, and which we reckoned on having been restored to us after the late enquiry, will be impaired.

"From the enquiry we have gained great confidence, because the Government of India and the Secretary of State had intimated that, if the enquiry should bring to light no rights of occupancy, then Government will do nothing; and we also felt assured of this, that the honesty of our purpose could not be proved by any arguments so strongly as by an enquiry thus made, and the result of the enquiry was, that the cultivators of the districts reported to the Financial Commissioner that there were no occupancy rights, and the Financial Commissioner reported to the same effect to Government. We hoped that we should be relieved of all further anxiety on the score of occupancy rights.

"But the result is, that the present proposal has been made, to which if we agree, we apprehend great harm to our former rights, and the rights secured by our sunuds, from the interference of Government.

"Therefore, we pray that the promise made by the Secretary of State and the Government of India—that if there are rights of occupancy they will be maintained, otherwise not—may be fulfilled, for the officers, after full enquiry, have found no such right."

Here the negociations ended. On the issue fixed by the

Secretary of State as the object of the late enquiry, *viz.*, whether rights of occupancy existed in Oudh before Annexation, Mr. Davies had found that no length of occupancy maintained by a ryot under the native Government gave him a right to hold against the will of the proprietor. The natural and logical deduction from this finding was, that all non-proprietary cultivators in Oudh were mere tenants-at-will. The taluqdars, therefore, prayed the Government that *all* non-proprietary cultivators, be they ex-proprietors or their descendants, should be recorded and treated as tenants-at-will. Nothing short of this, they respectfully submitted, would redeem the pledge given by the Secretary of State and the Government of India, that if the result of the late enquiry should be to prove that no rights of occupancy existed before Annexation, none would be created. No interference in any shape whatever must be exercised to prevent a proprietor doing what he pleased with the land in the occupation of a tenant-at-will, and if any interest whatever in the land is given to the latter independent of the proprietor, a *new right* would be created, and the promise made by the Secretary of State and the Government of India would be broken; and this the taluqdars most respectfully deprecated.

In March 1866, Sir Charles Wingfield retired from service, and Sir John Strachey was appointed Chief Commissioner. After Sir Charles Wingfield's departure no attempt was made for some time to reopen the negociations, the failure of which was reported to the India Government by the late Chief Commissioner. In May 1866, the new Chief Commissioner, Sir John Strachey, wrote a demi-official letter to Mr. Grey on the subject: "I have a strong conviction," he wrote to say, "that so far as the great mass of cultivators are concerned, there is only one possible solution to this question of tenant-right in Oudh. What that solution is, I have endeavoured to show in the accompanying note. You will understand from what you know of my opinions, that the conclusions which I have expressed have not been come to very willingly, and I suppose that Mr. Davies (who entirely agreed with him) has felt this still more strongly. But it seems to me that the time has clearly passed by in which anything was to be gained by

Sir John Strachey.

discussions as to the economical advantages and disadvantages of certain lines of policy. I find certain facts, which I must accept, whether I like them or not. I have endeavoured, therefore, to take a purely practical view of this question, and it is from this point of view that I come to the conclusion that the course I recommend the Government to adopt is inevitable.

"If I am right in this opinion, I think that the measures which I propose cannot be carried out too soon. At the present time it is still possible for the Government to close this long pending question without any loss of its own dignity, but it is still clear to me that this will not be possible much longer. After careful enquiry into the matter, I confidently expect, if Government will adopt the course I have proposed, that I shall be able to induce the taluqdars, without difficulty, to agree to grant to the class of dispossessed proprietors terms which the Government will think quite fair and satisfactory.

"I cannot express too strongly my opinion of the necessity of bringing this question to a close with the least possible delay. I have seen enough of Oudh already to convince me that all delay in settlement must exercise a most pernicious influence upon the province. I hear from many quarters of the bad feeling between landlords and tenants to which the discussion of these questions has given, and is still giving rise, and the tenants being the weaker party will be the chief sufferers."

He, therefore, strongly urged on the India Government to accept the proposals which he made, and to bring speedily these controversies to an end. He appended to this a very valuable note on Tenant Right in Oudh, from which we give the following extracts :—

"It has been declared by the Secretary of State and by the Government of India, that no rights of occupancy on the part of non-proprietary cultivators can be admitted, unless it be proved that such rights existed at the time of Annexation. 'The only foundation on which they can rest, is their previous existence at the time of Annexation.' These are the words of the Secretary of State in his Despatch of the 10th February 1865, and it was distinctly declared that the late enquiry was instituted for the sole purpose of ascertaining whether such rights existed at the time of Annexation or not.

"As to the main result of that enquiry there is not much difference of opinion. The Government of India has declared itself satisfied that 'under the native Government of Oudh, there was vested in the ryot no right of occupancy which could be successfully maintained against the will of the landlord.'

"It has now to be determined by Government what course is to be followed.

"In the letter from the Foreign Secretary to Government, dated the 16th February 1866, it is stated that the rules which have been in force in Oudh since the Annexation of the province have recognized the existence of the rights of occupancy under certain circumstances; and it is proposed that these rules shall remain in force, and that the system which has hitherto been followed shall be maintained.

"This course seems to me to be clearly impracticable, because it is inconsistent with the orders issued by the Secretary of State and by the Government of India, when the late enquiry was undertaken, and which have been referred to in the first paragraph of this note. It having been declared that the present existence of rights of occupancy can rest upon nothing but their previous existence at the time of Annexation, it is impossible now to alter the ground and to say that it rests upon the fact that such rights have been acknowledged since Annexation. Orders of the Local Administration or of the Government recognizing such rights may have been valuable as evidence of fact while the late enquiry was going on, but they have now ceased to have any bearing upon the question at issue. It having been declared that these rights did not exist at the time of Annexation, the conclusion seems to me to be inevitable that the maintenance of these rules by the executive Government is impossible. The only way in which they could be maintained would be either by the will of the landlords or by fresh legislation.

"So far at least as the great mass of cultivators are concerned (for, as I shall notice presently, there is an important class to whom this does not necessarily apply), it seems to me to be clearly impracticable that anything should now be done to convert into actual rights of occupancy any usages by which they have commonly remained in possession of the land which they cultivate. It cannot be expected that the landlords should voluntarily admit the existence of rights which they, rightly or wrongly, undoubtedly believe to be adverse to their own interests. The late demi-official negociations have, if proof be wanted, shown distinctly that they will not do so. And it must be added, for it is an important element in the question, that the landlords, in refusing the concessions of such rights, would undoubtedly have at the present time the support of public opinion both in India and at Home.

"It seems to me equally clear that legislation for the purpose of giving to the ryots rights of occupancy, which it has been determined they did not possess at the time of Annexation, is, under existing circumstances, practically quite impossible.

"It is, I think, useless now to discuss whether these results are good or bad. Personally I regret them, and think them very unfortunate; but I look upon them as facts which can by no possibility be avoided, and I am, therefore, prepared fully to accept them. I consider that, whether we like it or not, there can only be one conclusion to this matter. Sooner or later the Government will be obliged to admit, as a necessary consequence of the enquiry that has been made, and of the engagements that have been entered into, that rights of occupancy on the part of ordinary cultivators in Oudh have no existence, and that all rules and orders which have hitherto recognized such rights must be cancelled. If this be so, the only wise course which the Government can now follow is, I think, fully and frankly to admit the fact. It is now in the power of Government to close this controversy, if not in a manner which it considers really satisfactory, at least without any loss to its dignity. If there be much more delay, and if the Government attempt to avoid what is inevitable, the result will, I am sure, be not only failure, but discredit to Government. Another result may probably be, that it will become impracticable to do anything to improve the position of one class of cultivators whose claims to consideration are specially strong, and whose case is at present far from hopeless.

"This class is that which consists of ancient proprietors and their descendants—men whose forefathers were the undoubted owners of the land, and who, although they have lost or become despoiled of their proprietary rights, still retain possession of their ancestral fields. Whatever be the legal position which these men now hold, it will, I think, be generally allowed that their case is in many respects a very different one from that of other classes of cultivators. There is an almost universal feeling that they have strong equitable claims to consideration, and the propriety is commonly admitted of doing for them anything which can fairly be done without undue interference. This was in fact admitted by Mr. Wingfield himself, when, in the late demi-official negociations, he advised the taluqdars to grant on certain conditions favorable terms to these old proprietors. To a great extent it is certainly true that this feeling is that of the landlords themselves, and it is my belief that they may be induced, without much difficulty, to agree to any reasonable plan for protecting the equitable rights of this class of cultivators. Further, I believe, that if this anticipation be disappointed, public opinion would support the Government in any fair and moderate measures which it might be thought necessary to carry out by legislation. I do not at all anticipate that such interference by legislation would be required, but I see no reason for doubting that, by one means or the other, everything which the Government is likely to desire for this class of cultivators can be effected.

"In the demi-official negociations which were carried on with the taluqdars just before Mr. Wingfield left Oudh, it was proposed that a compromise should be effected. The taluqdars, on the one hand, were to grant certain favorable conditions to the dispossessed proprietors; the Government, on the other hand, was to admit that ordinary cultivators possessed no rights of occupancy. I need not refer more particularly to the proposed terms of the compromise, nor to the causes which led to the failure of the negociations. Those negociations having failed, I think it neither expedient nor dignified to attempt at present to reopen them.

"There is in fact, as it seems to me, no room now left for any compromise. I have stated in a previous part of this note my conviction, that, with regard to the great mass of cultivators, the Government would be obliged to admit that no rights of occupancy exist, and that all Circulars and Orders which recognize such rights must be cancelled. Whatever may hereafter be done for the dispossessed proprietors, this general conclusion seems to me inevitable. If this be the case, I think that the Government should now, without further reference to the taluqdars, do everything which it is prepared to do, and which ultimately it will be obliged to do. The Government will then be in its right position, and in a far stronger position than that which it now holds. It will then have a better right to hope that the taluqdars will take a liberal view of the claims of the class which the Government specially desires to protect, and if the taluqdars refuse to do so, it will then be open to the Government to consider what further measures it shall adopt. This course would be extremely popular. It would inspire great confidence in the Government on the part of the taluqdars, and while it sacrificed no rights which it is now possible to preserve, it would commend itself as just and straightforward to all classes of the public.

"The principle of the arrangement which I now advise has in fact been already admitted by the Government. In the late demi-official negociations, a course was agreed to by the Government which was equivalent to an admission on its part that ordinary cultivators possess no rights of occupancy capable of enforcement against the will of the landlord. This admission is not in reality less complete for having been accompanied by the proposal that the taluqdars should grant certain favorable terms to the dispossessed proprietors."

His recommendations.

Mr. Strachey then recommended that the following orders should now be issued :—

"*1st.*—The Government declares that the late enquiry has proved, that, at the time of Annexation, there was vested in the ryot no right of occupancy which could be successfully maintained against the will of the landlord. In accordance, therefore, with the promises made by the Secretary of State, and by the Government of India when the late enquiry was undertaken, the Government now declares that no new rights of occupancy will be created by the Government, and that the Government will not claim for non-proprietary cultivators any rights of occupancy based upon prescription, and not upon special contract. This declaration is to be held subject to the reservation in respect of ancient proprietors and their descendants, &c., &c., &c. * * * Mr. Grey has remarked that it might not be desirable to express this reservation, because he feared that this might seem to the taluqdars to be a qualification of the finality of the settlement which Government had proposed to make of the whole question. This seems to me to be quite true, and I think it undesirable and unnecessary to hold out any threats to the taluqdars of something that may happen, if a different state of things to the present should arise."

THE FINAL ADJUSTMENT.

It is not necessary to proceed any further with this discussion. Enough has been given to show that the tide had turned entirely in favor of the taluqdars. The rights of all classes of *proprietors* were fully recognized, and the alleged rights of occupancy of non-proprietary cultivators were acknowledged to be a myth. For the final adjustment of the tenant-right question, the reader is referred to the correspondence and orders, published at the time in the *Gazette of India* (September 1, 1866) here quoted *in extenso.**

* GOVERNMENT OF INDIA, FOREIGN DEPARTMENT.

Rights of Occupancy in Oudh.

From J. STRACHEY, ESQ., *Chief Commissioner of Oudh, to the* HON'BLE W. MUIR, *Secretary to the Government of India, Foreign Department, dated Simla, the 20th August* 1866.

In my demi-official letter to the Hon'ble Mr. Grey, dated the 9th June 1866, on the subject of rights of occupancy in Oudh, I stated my belief that the matters at issue might be more easily disposed of, if the question of sub-settlements were brought to a conclusion at the same time. In the minds of the taluqdars these two questions are closely connected with each other, and I expressed the hope that, by taking them up together, it might be possible to arrive at an arrangement which would be satisfactory both to the Government

At tne end of August 1866 then the vexed question of tenant-right in Oudh was finally concluded, apparently to the satisfac-

---

and to the taluqdars. In accordance with the authority which I subsequently received, I have, for some time past, been engaged, in concert with the Financial Commissioner, Mr. Davies, with Colonel Barrow, the Commissioner of Lucknow, and with Maharajah Maun Singh and other principal taluqdars of the Province, in drawing up plans for the final settlement of both these questions. Having arrived at conclusions which appeared to me to be satisfactory, I then, with the permission of His Excellency the Governor-General, proceeded to Simla, in the belief that I might be able, by personal explanation, to remove any difficulties which might still remain. Having been allowed by His Excellency to discuss fully with him all the questions that are at issue, I now submit the following propositions for the orders of the Government.

2. I do not now propose to enter into any fresh discussion of these subjects. The whole of the facts are already known to the Government, and it appears that all that it is now necessary for me to do, is to lay before the Government, as briefly as possible, practical recommendations which may lead to the final settlement of these questions, which have been so long under consideration.

3. It will be convenient to speak first of the question of sub-settlements. The proposals which I wish to make upon this subject are contained in the draft rules, Appendix A. A few remarks and explanations will, it is hoped, make them easily intelligible.

4. The first two rules contain nothing that is new. The principles which they lay down are in accordance with the views expressed by the late Chief Commissioner, Sir Charles Wingfield, and they have already been generally approved by the Government. They declare that the extension of the term of limitation for the hearing of claims to under-proprietary rights in land has made no change in the principles hitherto observed in the recognition of rights to sub-settlement. If an under-proprietor has enjoyed no rights during the period of limitation, beyond the possession of certain lands as *Seer* or *Nankar*, he will be entitled to the recognition of a proprietary right in those lands, but not to a sub-settlement of the village. To entitle him to a sub-settlement of the village, he must show that he has held with some degree of continuousness, by virtue of his under-proprietary right, a contract for the management since the village was included in the taluqa.

5. Rule 3 is a new one. It defines the meaning which is ordinarily to be attached to the word "some degree of continuousness." The diversity of practice has hitherto been great, and experience has shown it to be essentially necessary that an arbitrary rule should be laid down for the guidance of the Settlement Courts. The proposed rule has, at first sight, a somewhat complicated appearance, but in reality it is very simple. It amounts to this,—(*1st*), that no enquiries will be made regarding any lease that may have been held before the 13th February 1836,—that is, more than twenty years before the annexation of the Province; (*2nd*), that the lease must have been held for one year more than half of the period that may have elapsed between the time at

tion of all parties. After recording his views on the policy of Lord Canning in Oudh, and the probable effect of that policy on

---

which the village was included in the taluqa and Annexation: and (3*rd*), that, unless the village was, for the first time, included in the taluqa after the 13th February 1844, the lease must have been held for seven out of the last twelve years before Annexation. This rule is liable to exception in certain cases in which it would operate harshly. Cases in which a village was included for the first time in the taluqa, during the term of limitation, and in which the under-proprietor has held no lease for any period under the taluqdar, have not been provided for by this rule. Regarding these cases I proposed to address the Government hereafter. The proposed rule, although less favorable to the under-proprietors than that which has lately been followed in some cases, is very much more favorable to them than the rules contained in the Oudh Circ lars which have hitherto been considered to be in force.

6. Rules 4 and 5 are quite in accordance with the spirit of the rules that have hitherto been acted upon; but it has been considered desirable, for the protection of the under-proprietors, to lay down more definitely the procedure to be followed in the classes of cases to which the rules refer. It is provided by Rule 4 that if an under-proprietor, who is entitled to a sub-settlement, can show that he had entered into a written agreement with the taluqdar to hold the contract for the village at a uniform rate of payment in perpetuity, he will not be liable to any enhancement of rent during the currency of the present settlement, nor will the payment be increased at any future time unless the re-adjustment of the Government demand should alter the proportion between the respective shares of the profits derived from the land by the under-proprietor and by the taluqdar. In this case the rent payable by the under-proprietor will be liable to readjustment, so that the proportion between the shares of the two parties may remain unchanged. Rule 5 provides for cases in which the under-proprietor paid no more before the annexation of the Province than the Government demand, with the addition of certain dues, or other charges, to the taluqdar. In such cases the former custom will be maintained. The under-proprietor will never pay more than the Government demand, with the addition of 10 per cent. in lieu of dues and other charges.

7. Rule 6 provides for cases in which the under-proprietor and the taluqdar have shared the profits or produce of the village in a certain fixed proportion. In such cases the former custom will be maintained. This rule, although a new one, is quite in accordance with the system that has hitherto been followed, and it is evidently equitable.

8. Rule 7 provides for the regulation of the payments of the under-proprietor to the taluqdar in cases not falling under Rules 5 and 6. This rule, like those that precede it, is based on the principle which has always hitherto been followed in Oudh, that the payments made by the under-proprietor to the taluqdar before Annexation will form the standard by which the present payments are to be regulated. I need not now refer in detail to the reasons which, since the re-occupation of the Province in 1858, have led to the uniform adop-

the comfort and contentment of the people, the Governor-General frankly said (September 16, 1866) that he "fully

---

tion of this principle in determining the amount of the payments which are to be made by the under-proprietors to the taluqdars. The principle is of course a very different one from that which has been followed under our revenue system in other Provinces, and it is much more favorable to the taluqdars. The facts are well known to the Government, and it is sufficient to say here that the system which has hitherto been followed in Oudh, and which it is now proposed to perpetuate, has its origin in the engagements entered into with the taluqdars by Sir Robert Montgomery when their estates were restored to them on the re-occupation of the Province in 1858. I think that no other system could now be adopted without exposing the Government to the charge of having broken faith with the taluqdars. If the former and the present gross rental of the village be approximately the same. the payments of the under-proprietor to the taluqdar will remain unaltered. If the present gross rental exceed or fall short of the former gross rental, the payments of the under-proprietors will be proportionally increased or diminished. These rules are in accordance with the intention of those which have hitherto been in force, but the old rules were not very intelligibly expressed, and they were liable to be misunderstood. The cases are very few in which the former rental and the former payments cannot be ascertained with sufficient correctness for practical purposes. I have thought it sufficient at present to lay down the general principles by which the payments of the under-proprietors are to be regulated. There will be no difficulty in drawing up hereafter any supplementary rules that may be required.

9. Rule 8 is a new one. It provides for cases in which the share of the profits of the village. which the under-proprietor is entitled to receive, is so small that it is obviously not for his interest that the sub-settlement should be made. If his clear share of the profit do not exceed 12 per cent., it is proposed that, instead of obtaining a sub-settlement, he will be entitled to receive *Seer* and *Nankar* land of such value that his total profit shall not fall below one-tenth of the gross rental. He will possess in this land a complete transferable and heritable right of property. This arrangement is a very beneficial one for the under-proprietors, and at the same time it is one that will be liked by the taluqdars. The principle upon which this rule is founded will be further explained in the next paragraph.

10. Rule 9 is also new. It provides that if the share of the gross rental to which an under-proprietor is entitled exceeds 12, but falls short of 25 per cent., it shall be made up to the latter amount, the charge falling half upon the Government and half upon the taluqdar. The principle upon which this rule is based is this,—the taluqdars are bound by the conditions of their sunuds to maintain all holding under them "in the possession of all the subordinate rights they formerly enjoyed." An under-proprietor who is entitled to the sub-settlement of a village, but whose share of the profits is small, will, undoubtedly if we make a sub-settlement with him for a term of thirty years,

accepted the settlement of the Oudh arrangements" made by Mr. Strachey with his sanction. "I have no desire whatever,"

---

and oblige him to pay the same amount which he paid to the taluqdar before the annexation of the Province, be placed. as a general rule, in a worse position than that which he held under the native Government. Under our system a single bad season may easily complete his ruin; for if he fail to pay punctually the amount due to the taluqdar, his tenure being a heritable and transferable property may be brought to sale in satisfaction of a summary decree. No such penalties attached under the native Government to default of payment, and we have no right to place the under-proprietor in a worse position than that which he formerly held; consequently, he ought to receive such an increase to his share of the profits as will compensate him for the injury done to him. It is considered that this object will be gained in an equitable manner by the proposed rule. It would not be right to throw the whole burden upon the taluqdar, because it has been by the introduction of our own revenue system that the position of the under-proprietors has been injured. On the other hand it is right that the taluqdar should bear a portion of the charge, because he will otherwise be placed in a better position than that in which we have agreed to maintain him. The proposal is that the Government and the taluqdar shall share between them the charge on this account. The maximum possible loss in any single case to the Government will be 6 per cent. on the rental. but it will only reach this amount in extreme and exceptional cases, and it will usually be much less. It is not believed that the loss of revenue to the Government can possibly be anything serious, nor will the adoption of this rule affect the fact that the revision of settlement now in progress in Oudh will lead to a very large increase in the Government demand. It should also be remembered that it was distinctly admitted by Lord Canning, that some sacrifice of the Government revenue might result from the system that was established in Oudh in 1858. The recognition of two classes of proprietors in one estate was stated in the orders of the Government of India, No. 23, dated 19th October 1859, to be "likely to lead to the alienation of a larger proportion of the land-revenue than if there were only one such class." The same fact was admitted in the orders passed upon the Record of Rights Circular by the Government of India, No. 74, dated 8th January 1861. Although in these orders the Government only contemplated the case in which it would be proper to increase the share of the taluqdar, and did not refer to the necessity of some times increasing the share of the under-proprietor, it appears clear that the principle laid down by the Government is just as applicable in the one case as in the other.

11. Rule 10 is in exact accordance with the practice hitherto followed in Oudh. An under-proprietor, who is not entitled to a sub-settlement but who has retained possession of *Seer* or *Nankar* land, is held to possess in such land a complete right of property, subject to the payment to the taluqdar, in perpetuity, of the rent that is due. The provisions of the existing rules are extremely favourable to the under-proprietors, and as they have always been acted upon, it is proposed to maintain them. But it seems to me

he added, "that they should again be brought under discussion; and I sincerely hope that they will protect, and conduce to,

---

questionable whether they are altogether compatible with the complete security of the Government revenue. I propose to consider this subject separately.

12. Rule 11 gives, under certain circumstances, to persons who have founded *poorwas*, or hamlets, the same privileges which are given to under-proprietors by Rule 10. No definite rules have hitherto been laid down on this subject.

13. Rule 12 requires no remark. It provides that claims to proprietary and under-proprietary rights in jagheers will be treated according to the same rules which are applicable to similar claims in taluqas.

14. Rule 13 provides that claims to under-proprietary rights, which may have been disposed of already in a manner not in accordance with these rules, will be opened to revision, unless they have been settled by arbitration or agreement of parties.

15. Except in the cases in which they contain new provisions, these rules are generally in accordance with those laid down, or proposed by the late Chief Commissioner, Sir Charles Wingfield. The Financial Commissioner considers that, to enable some portions of the rules to be carried out, legislation will be necessary; but with this reservation I believe that the whole of them will meet Mr. Davies's approval. I have also communicated the proposed rules to Maharajah Maun Singh and the Committee by which the business of the taluqdars is conducted. The Maharajah and the Committee, having been duly empowered by the taluqdars to act in this matter as their representatives, have authorized me to state to the Government that the taluqdars would gladly accept these rules as providing a satisfactory solution of the questions which have so long been pending.

16. There is only one other matter, connected with the subject of sub-settlements, to which I think it now necessary to refer. The opinion was expressed by Lord Canning that "it is a bad principle to create two classes of recognized proprietors in one estate."* I believe that the truth of this opinion cannot be denied. Although, when the right to sub-settlement is proved, it could not justly be withheld, unless complete compensation were given for its surrender, it appears to me clear that all sub-settlements are, in principle, economically bad. I think that, subject to such restrictions and conditions as the Financial Commissioner may prescribe, all Settlement Officers might, with much advantage, be told that if in any case they can induce the taluqdar and the under-proprietor to agree amicably to a separation of their respective properties, so that each of them shall retain a complete right of property over a portion of the estate instead of an incomplete right of property over the whole, the Government will look upon such a result as one that is beneficial, not only to the parties immediately concerned, but to the country generally.

17. There is one other class of cases which I may properly notice here although I am not now able to propose that any final orders should be given

---

* Letter to Chief Commissioner of Oudh, No. 23, dated 19th October 1859.

the interests of all classes from the taluqdar to the humblest tiller of the soil, and thereby to the consolidation and security

---

regarding them. It sometimes happened that a village which had long formed a well-recognized portion of a taluqa and which had been held by the taluqdar during the greater part of the term of limitation, was for some reason or other not in his actual possession when the Province was annexed, and has been excluded from his sunud. The period of limitation for hearing claims for the recovery of under-proprietary rights having been extended with the consent of the taluqdars, they consider that a similar privilege should equitably be given to them also, and that they should be allowed, in certain cases, to ask that the villages be re-included in their taluqas. They admit that this claim cannot always be admitted. The village, for example, may have been included in the sunud of another taluqdar, or the full proprietary right may have been given away by the Government to some other party. I am not prepared, without further enquiry, to make any final recommendation on this subject; but I think that I might be allowed to say this much to the taluqdars, that the Government considers that their request is fair in principle, and that there will be no objection to admitting it, provided that this does not lead to the infringement of the rights of any other parties.

18. I proceed to lay before the Government the following propositions for the settlement of the questions that are now pending regarding rights of occupancy in Oudh. I propose to follow a similar course to that which I have adopted in regard to the question of such settlements. I shall enter into no fresh discussion, but shall confine myself to practical recommendations for the final determination of the matters at issue.

19. I propose that, in the first place authority be given to me to make known to the taluqdars, and to the public generally, the following declaration of the views and intentions of the Government :—

(1.)– Considering that, by the enquiry which has lately been made into the subject of rights of occupancy in Oudh, it has been shown that, at the time of the annexation of the Province, there was vested in the ryot no right of occupancy which could be successfully maintained against the will of the landlord. The Government, in accordance with the engagements entered into by the Secretary of State and by the Government of India, when the late enquiry was undertaken, now declares that no rights of occupancy will be created by the Government.

(2.)—All orders, rules, and circulars which have hitherto been in force in Oudh recognizing a right or preference of occupancy in non-proprietary cultivators, will be cancelled.

(3.)—The rules, orders, and circulars which have hitherto been in force, in respect of the hearing of suits in the Summary Courts, will be revised, so that they may be brought into accordance with the present orders.

20. I propose to consider, in concert with the Financial Commissioner, the exact nature of the measures which it will be necessary to take with the object of carrying into complete effect the recommendations contained in the two last

of British influence in Oudh." These are noble sentiments, and are well worthy of a Viceroy, who was looked upon as the

---

clauses of the last preceding paragraph. I propose to address the Government on this subject hereafter.

21. If the foregoing propositions regarding the two questions of sub-settlement and rights of occupancy should be approved by the Government, I am authorized to lay before the Government on behalf of the taluqdars the following proposals:—

22. The taluqdars, although they have always denied the existence of any rights of occupancy in Oudh, are willing, as a matter of favor, though not of right, to grant to one class of cultivators certain privileges. This is the class of ancient proprietors of the soil, who, although they have lost all proprietary right, still occupy as cultivators land in their ancestral villages. These men very commonly hold their lands at favorable rates, and the taluqdars are willing to bestow upon them, as a right, advantages which they now hold by favor only. The conditions under which the taluqdars are prepared to make this concession are shown in the Memorandum (marked B) appended to this letter. A few remarks may properly be made regarding them.

23. The first proposal of the taluqdars contained in paragraph 2 of the Memorandum is to the following effect:—Every person who has been in possession of proprietary rights in a village, within the thirty years preceding the annexation of the Province, will be deemed to possess an hereditary right of occupancy in the land which he now cultivates in such village, provided that his possession, either by himself, or by some person from whom he has inherited, shall have lasted since the time at which he ceased to possess such proprietary rights, or continuously for twenty years.

24. Paragraphs 3 and 4 of the Memorandum do not require any special notice. Paragraph 5 contains the conditions under which the rent of an ex-proprietor having an hereditary right of occupancy will be liable to enhancement. These are taken with a few verbal alterations only from the draft of a Bill to amend Act X of 1859, drawn up by the Hon'ble Mr. Muir. It appears to me that these conditions, which need not be repeated here, are very appropriate, and they are entirely approved by the taluqdars. It will be within the recollection of the Government that the proposal of Sir Charles Wingfield was to the effect that this class of ex-proprietors should hold at a uniform rate of two annas in the rupee less than the rate of rent paid by tenants-at-will. In the majority of cases this will probably be the result of applying the provisions of Mr. Muir's Bill.

I propose to request the Financial Commissioner to consider what will be the best course to follow for recording the rights which will thus be bestowed upon the class of ex-proprietary cultivators.

25. Paragraphs 6 and 7 of the Memorandum are also taken from Mr. Muir's Bill. The former provides that, after the rent of an ex-proprietor with right of occupancy has been fixed in accordance with these rules, it will not again be

guardian and protector of the rights of all classes of Her Majesty's subjects in India. But we regret to say that the policy

---

liable to enhancement for five years,* except under certain circumstances. Paragraph 7 provides that no cultivator can claim an abatement of rent.

26. In paragraph 8 of the Memorandum, the taluqdars agree that if a landlord determine to oust from his holding any tenant not having a right of occupancy, the tenant will be entitled to claim compensation for any unexhausted improvements which have been made at his own expense, and by which the annual letting value of the land has been increased. This compensation will be payable in cash, but it will be at the option of the landlord, instead of making such payment, to offer to the tenant a lease on terms sufficiently favorable to reimburse him for his outlay.

Considering that, as a general rule, all improvements are made by the tenants, this provision will have a very important effect. It will, in practice, afford sufficient protection to every tenant who deserves any protection at all.

27. There are various other matters of detail which will have to be settled, but it is not now necessary to speak of them. Legislation may possibly be found necessary hereafter to confirm some of the proposed arrangements, but there need be no delay on this account, and there will be no present difficulty in putting them in force when they have been approved by the Government.

28. I wish to acknowledge the very great assistance which has been given to me by Mr. Davies, the Financial Commissioner, and by Colonel Barrow, the Commissioner of Lucknow, in bringing these difficult questions to a conclusion. I must at the same time say that any value which the results which been arrived at may possess is, in a very great measure, due to the excellent advice given by my predecessor to the taluqdars, shortly before his departure from India. I regret that Sir Charles Wingfield should not himself have had the satisfaction of bringing these questions to a conclusion before he left the Province, the affairs of which he had long administered with conspicuous ability. I believe that, although he may possibly doubt the propriety of some portions of the arrangements that have now been proposed, he will, upon the whole, consider them fair and satisfactory for all parties.

The Government will, I hope, be of opinion that the proposals which have been made by the taluqdars on the subject of rights of occupancy, are very creditable to them. The same may, I think, be said of the ready assent which they have given to the arrangements proposed in the matter of sub-settlements. I think that the taluqdars have shown in all the late proceedings a spirit of conciliation and liberality which deserves the acknowledgment of the Government. They have been fortunate in having as their chief leader and adviser a man of such remarkable intelligence as Maharajah Maun Singh.

29. I believe that if the propositions which have now been made be carried into effect, we may confidently hope to see a complete and an immediate termination to all the unfortunate dissensions and discussions by which, for so

---

* In Mr. Muir's Bill the term is ten years.

of Sir John with regard to the alleged rights of the cultivators of Oudh was not looked upon by the public, nay by his own

---

long a period, the Province of Oudh has been distracted. It would be unbecoming in me to comment upon the policy which has been followed by His Excellency the Governor-General in respect of these important questions. But considering the position which I hold, and remembering the criticisms to which recent measures in Oudh have been subjected, I think that I may say without impropriety that if those measures be judged by the results that have followed from them, they must be pronounced to have been completely successful. The importance on these questions is so great that, in all probability, the future fortunes of the Province will, for many generations to come, be strongly influenced by the manner in which they are decided. The final result of the measures taken by His Excellency the Governor-General will, I believe, be beneficial in the highest degree to the most important interests of the Province. The condition of the humbler classes of the agricultural community, upon whom in so great a degree the prosperity of the country depends, will have been rendered far better than it would otherwiso have been, while at the same time, the taluqdars will retain unimpaired the high position which was assigned to them by the Government of Lord Canning. If proof of this last assertion be wanted, it may be found in the fact that all these results will have been brought about, not only with the consent and approval of the taluqdars, but with their active help and co-operation.

APPENDIX A.

Rules regarding Sub-Settlement and other subordinate Rights of Property in Oudh.

The extension of the term of limitation for the hearing of claims to under-proprietary rights in land, makes of itself no alteration in the principles hitherto observed in the recognition of a right to sub-settlement.

2. When no rights are proved to have been exercised or enjoyed by an under-proprietor during the period of limitation, beyond the possession of certain lands as *Seer* or *Nankar*, no sub-settlement can be made; but the claimant will be entitled, in accordance with the rules contained in the Circular Orders which have hitherto been in force in Oudh upon this subject, to the recognition of a proprietary right in such land. To entitle a claimant to obtain a sub-settlement, he must show that he possesses an under-proprietary right in the lands of which the sub-settlement is claimed, and that such right has been kept alive over the whole area claimed within the period of limitation. He must also show that he, either by himself or by some other person or persons from whom he has inherited, has, by virtue of his under-proprietary right, and not merely through privilege granted on account of service, or by farm of the taluqdar, held such lands under contract (*pucka*), with some degree of continuousness since the village came into the taluqa.

colleagues in Council, in the same light in which he was anxious that it should be considered. But let that pass.

---

3. The words "some degree of continuousness" will be interpreted as follows:—

If the village was included in the taluqa before the 13th February 1836 the lease must have been held for not less than twelve years between that date and the annexation of the Province. If the village was included in the taluqa after the 13th February 1836, but before the 13th February 1844, the lease must have been held for not less than one year more than half the period between the time in which the village was so included and the annexation of the Province. Further, the lease must, in all cases, have been held for not less than seven years during the term of limitation, unless the village was included for the first time in the taluqa after the 13th February 1844, in which case the lease must have been held for not less than one year more than half of the period between the time in which the village was so included and the annexation of the Province. Provided, that if, for any reason, the taluqdar was, for any period, dispossessed of the village, and the under-proprietor was dispossessed from the lease during the same period, the term of such dispossession shall not be reckoned against the under-proprietor. Provided also, that nothing in this rule will apply to any village which was included for the first time in the taluqa after the 13th February 1844, and in which the under-proprietor has held no lease for any period under the taluqdar.

4. If an under-proprietor, who is entitled to a sub-settlement, can show by documentary evidence that he had entered into an agreement with the taluqdar that he should hold, in perpetuity, the lease of the lands to the sub-settlement of which he is entitled at a uniform (*istimraree*) rate of payment, and that such agreement has been acted on within the period of limitation, he will not be liable to payment at an increased rate during the currency of the present or revised settlement. If, in consequence of any future re-adjustment of the Government demand, the former proportion between the respective shares of the profits derived from the land by the under-proprietor and the taluqdar should be altered, the amount payable by the under-proprietor to the taluqdar will be liable to re-adjustment, so that the proportion between their respective shares of the profits may remain unaltered.

5. If an under-proprietor, entitled to sub-settlement, can show by documentary evidence that he had entered into an agreement with the taluqdar that he should hold the lease of the lands to the sub-settlement of which he is entitled, on payment of the Government demand imposed before the annexation of the Province on such lands, with the addition only of certain dues to the taluqdar or other charges, and such agreement has been acted upon within the period of limitation, such under-proprietor will, in future, be liable only for the payment to the taluqdar of the Government demand for the time being, with the addition of 10 per cent. in lieu of taluqdari dues and other charges.

6. If an under-proprietor, entitled to sub-settlement, has held the lease of the lands to the sub-settlement of which he is entitled, under an agreement

What followed is thus described by the *Englishman* (May 30, 1867): "We all know," says this leading organ of public

---

that he shall pay to the taluqdar a certain share or proportion of the profits or produce of such lands, and such agreement has been acted upon within the term of limitation, the under-proprietor will, in future, continue to be liable for the payment to the taluqdar of such share or proportion.

7. In all cases in which an under-proprietor is entitled to a sub-settlement other than those described in Rules 4 to 6, the amount payable by the under-proprietor to the taluqdar will be determined according to the following principles:—

1*st.*—The payments made by the under-proprietor to the taluqdar before Annexation will form the standard by which the present payments are to be regulated.

2*nd.*—In no case the amount payable by the under-proprietor to the taluqdar during the currency of the settlement exceed the gross rental of the village, less 10 per cent. in *Seer* or *Nankar* land.

3*rd.*—In no case can the amount payable during the currency of the settlement (*sic*) by the amount of the revised Government demand, with the addition of 10 per cent.

4*th.*—If the gross rental of the village before Annexation and at the present time be approximately the same, the under-proprietor will pay to the taluqdar the same amount which he paid before Annexation.

5*th.*—If the present gross rental of the village exceed or fall short of the former gross rental, the payment of the under-proprietor to the taluqdar will be adjusted according to the following rule;—*viz.*, as the former gross rental is to the former payment of the under-proprietor, so is the present gross rental to the present payment of the under-proprietor.

6*th.*—In determining the amount payable by the under-proprietor to the taluqdar under the two last preceding rules, the former gross rental and the former payment of the under-proprietor will be held to be the average amount of the gross rental, and the average amount of the former payments of the under-proprietor for the twelve years preceding Annexation, or for such portion of that time as the under-proprietor held a lease of the village from the taluqdar, or for such portion of that time as the necessary information may be obtained.

8. In any case in which the clear share of the profit to which the under-proprietor is entitled under the rules contained in the last preceding paragraph does not exceed 12 per cent. of the gross rental, no sub-settlement shall be made. In this case, the under-proprietor will retain all *Seer* and *Nankar* land, to which his right is established. If the profits derived from such land be less than one-tenth of the whole rental of the land to the sub-settlement of which the right was established, the taluqdar shall increase the amount of such land, so that the total profit to the under-proprietor shall not fall below one-tenth of the gross rental.

The under-proprietor will possess, in the whole of such land, a transferable and heritable right of property.

opinion, "the abortive attempt made by Sir John Lawrence to disturb the settlement made by Lord Canning, and to endea-

---

9. In any case in which an under-proprietor is entitled to a sub-settlement under the preceding rules, and in which the share of the gross rental which such under-proprietor is entitled to receive exceeds 12 per cent., but falls short of 25 per cent., such share will be increased, so that it shall not be less than 25 per cent. of the gross rental. The cost of such increase will be borne half by the Government and half by the taluqdar. In this case, the cesses on account of roads, schools, &c., amounting to 2½ per cent. on the Government demand, will be payable by the taluqdar, while the village expenses, including the allowances to the putwari and chowkidar, will be payable by the under-proprietor.

10. When a former proprietor, who is not entitled to a sub-settlement, has retained within the period of limitation, either by himself or by some other person or persons from whom he has inherited, possession of land which by virtue of his proprietary right he held as *Seer* or *Nankar* when he was in proprietary possession, he will be deemed in respect of such land to be an under-proprietor and will possess a heritable and transferable right of property therein, subject to the payment of such amount as may be due by him to the superior proprietor.

11. If, in any case, the founder of a *poorwa* or hamlet, who is unable to establish a right to sub-settlement, can show that, in consideration of having founded such *poorwa* or hamlet, he has held therein, within the period of limitation, possession of *Seer* or *Nankar* land, he will be recognized as an under-proprietor in such land, subject to the payment of such amount as may be due by him to the taluqdar. The amount of such payment will be determined according to the rules for determining the amount of the payments due by other under-proprietors on their *Seer* or *Nankar* lands.

12. Claims to proprietary and under-proprietary rights in jagheers, will be treated according to the same rules which are applicable to similar claims in taluqas.

13. Case in which claims to under-proprietary rights have been disposed of otherwise than in accordance with these rules will be open to revision, but this rule will not apply to cases disposed of by arbitration or by agreement of the parties.

J. STRACHEY,
Chief Commissioner of Oudh.

SIMLA,
The 20th August 1866.

APPENDIX B.

Memorandum on Rights of Occupancy in Oudh.

1. The following Memorandum shows the nature of the conditions under which the taluqdars are willing to grant certain privileges to certain classes of cultivators in Oudh.

vour to discover the existence of occupancy rights of cultivators in Oudh, and having discovered to recognize them to

---

It is to be understood that these concessions will only be agreed to on the understanding that the two questions of sub-settlement and of rights of occupancy have first been disposed of in a manner satisfactory to the taluqdars.

2. Every person, who, within thirty years preceding the annexation of the Province, has been either by himself, or by himself and some other person or persons from whom he has inherited, in possession of proprietary rights in a village or estate, will be deemed to possess an hereditary right of occupancy in the land which he now cultivates or holds in such village or estate, whether it be held under patta or not, so long as he pays the rent payable on account of the same; provided that the possession either by himself, or by himself and some other persons as aforesaid, shall have lasted since the time at which he or such person or persons ceased to possess such proprietary rights or continuously for not less than twenty years.

Where such ex-proprietors, having a right of occupancy, shall, with the consent of the proprietor, have exchanged any land, in respect to which such right exists, for any other land belonging to the same proprietor in the same village or estate, such varied occupancy shall be held to be a continuous occupancy.

3. One succession shall be accepted as evidence of possession for the period mentioned in the last preceding rule, unless the contrary be shown.

4. Nothing contained in the foregoing rules shall be held to affect the terms of any written contract for the cultivation of land, entered into between a proprietor and tenant, when such contract contains any express stipulation contrary to such rules.

5. No ex-proprietor, having an hereditary right of occupancy, shall be liable to an enhancement of the rent previously paid by him, except on some one of the following grounds, *viz.*:—

Case 1st.—That the rate of rent paid by such ex-proprietor is below the prevailing rate payable by the class of ex-proprietors for land of a similar description, and with similar advantages in the places adjacent.

Rule.—In this case the Court will enhance the rent of such ex-proprietor to the full rate so prevailing.

Case 2nd.—That the rent of such ex-proprietor has remained without enhancement from a period since which the money value of agricultural produce in the vicinity has risen, or has been enhanced in a proportion less than the rise of such money value, or otherwise than in consequence of such rise.

Explanation.—This case shall apply only where it may appear to the Court that the rents of similar lands belonging to the class of ex-proprietors in the neighbourhood have not adjusted themselves to the increased money value of the produce.

Rule.—Where this case applies, the Court will enhance the rent according to the method of proportion, that is, the increased rent will bear to the previous the great injury of the taluqdars—nay even to the destruction of their proprietary rights. We all know how manfully this

---

rent the same proportion as the existing money value of agricultural produce bears to the money value of such produce at some previous period since which the rent has not been enhanced. In determining present or former standards of price, the Court shall, if possible, take the average of the prices for periods of not less than five years. It shall be competent to the Local Government to frame instructions for the ascertainment of the money value of agricultural produce for the purposes of this rule, and to publish standards of local prices, former and present, for the assistance of the Courts in carrying out this rule.

Case 3rd.—That the rent paid by such ex-proprietor is more than 12½ per cent. lower than the rent of land of a similar description and with similar advantages in the places adjacent, paid by cultivators not having the right of occupancy.

Explanation—Where no prevailing rate may be ascertainable under Case I, or where no personal title is proved to hold at a special rate, and the present rent is not shown to be fair and equitable, the rate of rent paid for similar land by cultivators not having a right of occupancy, minus 12½ per cent., shall be held to be a fair and equitable rate, provided such rate, is not below the rent actually paid.

Rule.—In this case the Court shall decree an enhancement, such as will raise the rent to the level of the rent assessable at the rates paid by cultivators not having the right of occupancy or land of a similar description and with similar advantages in the places adjacent, minus 2½ per cent.

Case 4th.—That the produce or productive power of the land has been increased, otherwise than by the agency or at the expense of the ex-proprietor.

Rule.—In this case, claims for enhancement may be adjusted in either of the following ways:—

(A)—By the Rules under Case I or under Case III (as the case may be) wherever it may appear that the rent of land in the vicinity of a similar description, and possessing similar advantages, has generally adjusted itself with a due reference to such advantages.

(B)—Where no such general adjustment is found to have taken place, or where it may not be possible to declare rates under Cases I and III, the Court shall enhance the rent by the whole value of the increased produce, or of the fairly-estimated result of the increased productive power, after deducting such amount, being not less than 20 per cent., in consideration of the increased responsibilities, expense, or labor of the ex-proprietor, as may appear to the Court equitable.

Case 5th.—That the quantity of land held by the ex-proprietor has been proved by measurement to be greater than the quantity for which rent has been previously paid by him.

Rule.—In this case the Court shall decree rent for the surplus land calculated at the same rates as those paid for the rest of the holding, or, if so claimed by the plaintiff, at rates to be fixed by the Rules under Case I or Case III foregoing.

attempt was resisted by Sir Charles Wingfield, and that this vexed question was settled by Mr. Strachey and the taluqdars;

General Proviso.—The rent of no ex-proprietor having the right of occupancy shall be liable to enhancement by reason only of improvements caused by or at the expense of such ex-proprietor; and where enhancement may be claimable on other grounds, a ratable allowance shall be made in favor of the ex-proprietor for any improvements effected by him or at his expense.

The words "places adjacent" in this Rule may be taken to signify such extent of country in the vicinity as, in the judgment of the Court, may reasonably be included in the investigation for the purpose of asserting the prevailing standard of rent.

6. After a decision passed in accordance with these Rules fixing an enhanced rent, or a fair and equitable rent, no suit shall lie for enhancement of the same, until the expiration of five years from the date of such decision excepting under Cases IV and V.

7. No claim for abatement of rent, on the ground that the rate hitherto paid is higher than that paid by other cultivators, shall be heard in any Court.

8. If a landlord determine to oust from his holding any tenant not having a right of occupancy, such tenant may claim from the landlord compensation for the value of any unexhausted improvements, such as wells, bunds, tanks, clearing jungles, and the like, which have been made at the expense of such tenant, and by which the annual letting value of the land has been increased. Such compensation will be payable in cash; but it shall be at the option of the landlord, instead of making such payment, to offer to such tenant a lease (*patta*) on terms sufficiently favorable to reimburse him for his outlay. In determining the amount of such compensation, account shall be taken of any assistance that may have been given by the landlord to the tenant when the improvement was made. In case of any dispute regarding the amount of compensation to be paid, or regarding the terms of the lease given in lieu thereof, the matter in dispute will be settled by the Revenue Court. Provided that nothing in this Rule shall affect the terms of any special agreement in writing, which may be made between a landlord and tenant regarding the making of improvements.

J. STRACHEY,
Chief Commissioner of Oudh.

From the HON'BLE WILLIAM MUIR, Secretary to the Government of India, Foreign Department, to the CHIEF COMMISSIONER, OUDH,—(No. 307, dated Simla, the 24th August 1866).

I have received, and submitted to the Right Hon'ble the Governor-General in Council, your letter dated the 20th instant, with enclosures, being a proposal made in concert with the taluqdars of Oudh, for the disposal of the questions now pending as to sub-proprietary settlements, and the position of tenants under taluqdars.

the latter, of their own free will, making concessions to the cultivators of the soil, which could never have been legally or

---

2. The latter subject has been now under discussion for a period of two years. Shortly before his departure from Oudh, an attempt was made by the late Chief Commissioner, Sir Charles Wingfield, to effect a compromise with the taluqdars on the basis of protecting alone the ex-proprietary tenantry—the class possessing the strongest claims upon the consideration of the British Government. The attempt failed. But you were authorized by the Viceroy and Governor-General to renew the negotiation, should the taluqdars be found ready to accept any reasonable compromise.

3. It has been known to His Excellency for sometime, from your demi-official communications, that the settlement of the above question was intimately connected in the mind of the taluqdars with another subject, *viz.*, the terms upon which sub-proprietors should be admitted to settlement under the taluqdars (a question which has also been under discussion with Government within the last year), that the taluqdars felt this question to be a matter more closely and vitally affecting their position and interests than that of cultivating occupancy; and that the latter might without much difficulty be disposed of, if the former were settled upon a satisfactory and equitable basis. Both subjects having been fully discussed by you with the body of the taluqdars, and principles of adjustment fair to all the parties concerned having been agreed to by the taluqdars, the Governor-General invited you to visit Simla in order that, in personal conference with His Excellency, the details of the proposed arrangement might be conclusively determined. Maharajah Maun Singh and two others of the taluqdars,* accompanied you. And His Excellency has accordingly had the satisfaction of carefully considering the whole subject, its different bearings as regards the State, the taluqdars, the sub-proprietors, and the cultivators of the land, in communication with yourself and the deputation of taluqdars.

4. The Governor-General sees much reason to conclude that the arrangements thus determined by consent are as fair and just to all parties as the peculiar circumstances of the Province will admit, and that they contain nothing which militates against the policy of Lord Canning, or which that statesman would not himself have cordially approved. Holding this view, and believing it to be of great importance that these questions should be set at rest with the least possible delay, His Excellency was pleased to intimate to yourself, and to the deputation from the taluqdars, that the principles and arrangements as above agreed on, and as set forth in your letter under reply, were accepted and confirmed by His Excellency.

5. I am now commanded by His Excellency in Council to communicate to you the formal sanction of the Governor-General in Council to the various measures detailed in your letter and its enclosures.

6. As regards sub-settlements, the basis upon which the opposing claims and conflicting interests of the two classes has been adjusted is, that the State shall make some sacrifice of its ordinary and legitimate dues in favour of the

---

* Chowdree Nawab Ally Khan, Bahadoor, and Tujummul Hossain Khan.

fairly wrested from them. All this we knew, but we were not prepared for the display of a bold independence on the part of

---

taluqdars, wherever, under the rules of assessment hitherto in force in such cases, an inadequate profit would have been left to the sub-proprietors. And that the taluqdars on their part shall, under the same circumstances, resign a proportion of their rental equal to that given up by the State; or that they will allow a moderate maintenance to the excluded sub-proprietors in the shape of land (*Nankar of do-biswai*) to be held rent-free or on light rent rates, in lieu of all further claims of a proprietary nature in the soil.

7. And, secondly, in consideration of this settlement and the advantage accruing to them therefrom, the taluqdars have voluntarily consented to make certain important concessions in respect of tenant-right. They have agreed to recognize the right of occupancy on beneficial terms in a large body of the ex-proprietary class—tillers of the lands, once owned by themselves or by their ancestors. The concession likewise embraces the interests of such cultivators as have settled hamlets, have reclaimed wastes, or have added by improvements to the selling value of their fields. The terms thus settled will embrace, in their aggregate, a large body of the cultivators of the Province, and of those classes especially which claim most strongly the sympathy and interest of the British Government. The liberal policy thus inaugurated by the taluqdars themselves will, in the long run, as His Excellency in Council feels assured, redound to their own interests by the important impetus to the improvement of their estates which will follow on the acquisition by the ryots of a better title; while it will tend to the contentment and the comfort of the cultivators themselves.

8. You are accordingly authorized by the Viceroy and Governor-General in Council to promulgate throughout the Province the rules proposed by you as the basis upon which the settlement operations, and the administration generally, will henceforth be conducted, and as the ground upon which all questions connected with the land-tenures of Oudh will be decided. All rules and circulars inconsistent with the new arrangements thus sanctioned will be rescinded and modified as may be found necessary. The sanction now conveyed to you embraces the proposals and the explanations of the several rules embodied in your letter.

9. In conclusion, I am to tender to you the hearty acknowledgments of the Government of India for the ability and judgment with which you have brought to a satisfactory conclusion questions of so difficult and complicated a character. You will also communicate to Mr. Davies, the Judicial Commissioner, and to Colonel Barrow, the Commissioner of Lucknow, the thanks of the Government for their aid and good services in bringing this result about.

10. The Government of India is deeply sensible of the praiseworthy and enlightened behaviour of the taluqdars of Oudh which has enabled you to reach so successful a conclusion. And you will not fail to inform the whole body of the taluqdars, and Maharajah Maun Singh in particular, how highly their conduct has been appreciated by the Viceroy and Governor-General in Council.

some of the members of the Council, which has not been surpassed by the most independent and free-spoken statesmen of England, and which must have galled and surprised in an equal degree the Governor-General of India. Mr. William Grey, the present Lieutenant-Governor of Bengal, shines conspicuous in the controversy, and he tells Sir John Lawrence, who, throughout the discussion, pretended that he only wished to discover whether such rights existed or not, that his intention was very different, and that had not the Chief Commissioner stood in the way, those rights would most certainly have been introduced into Oudh in 1864 without any *enquiry* on the assumption of their existence." The paragraph is worthy of quotation:—

'Though the Governor-General was afterwards induced to abandon this proposal, and in place of it to order an enquiry as to the existence in Oudh of occupancy rights of cultivators, on the ground that no sufficient enquiry had been made concerning the fact of their existence, and though there are occasional expressions to be found throughout the correspondence disclaiming any intention to *create* rights; and though the final instructions of September 30th do in express terms say that what was sought for was "the recognition of cultivating rights, provided their existence is judicially established," such recognition, it was justly argued, involving no departure from the sunuds given by Lord Canning to the taluqdars, yet it seems to me impossible to deny that there was an absolute foregone conclusion that the rights did exist; and that unless the Chief

---

11. While the Governor-General in Council anticipates that the rules now sanctioned will work equitably for all parties, it is yet possible that there may be some classes of cases, not here provided for, in respect of which this expectation may not reasonably be fulfilled. Should any such hereafter occur, His Excellency in Council trusts that you will, in communication with the taluqdars, be able to apply a suitable remedy in the spirit of the present arrangements; and the Governor-General does not doubt that the taluqdars, who have on this occasion shown so liberal and conciliatory a spirit, would again, in a like spirit, aid you, should such a contingency arise.

12. Your letter with its enclosures, and this reply, will be published in the *Gazette of India*.

W. MUIR,
Secy. to the Govt. of India.

Commissioner stood in the way, they would most certainly have been introduced into Oudh in 1864, without any enquiry into the assumption of their existence.'

And he further says :—

'I have ventured, in the above remarks, to state frankly my view of the question which was really put in issue as regards tenant-right in Oudh, when His Excellency the Governor-General first took up the subject, because I think it is only due to the late Chief Commissioner, Sir Charles Wingfield, that it should clearly appear what it was that compelled him to regard it as a duty to oppose the wishes of Government—an attitude which no public servant can ever wish to take up, unless upon a very strong conviction that the upholding of right and justice requires him to do so.'

"Sir Henry Durand follows suit, and fairly tells the Governor-General that there was no necessity for his meddling with the subject, and that the result of such meddling would be defeat; and as matters stood, 'Government were pretty sure to incur the rather humiliating result of having need essly incurred the suspicion of the taluqdars.' He concludes his Minute as follows : —'I remain very painfully under the impression that the general result is not such as to leave the Government, as compared with the behaviour of the taluqdars, in a satisfactory and dignified position. It would have been, in my opinion, infinitely preferable to have avoided altogether a protracted conflict, for the close of which, in a manner not *altogether* derogatory to Government, we are more indebted to the liberal and, under the circumstances, rather magnanimous concession of the taluqdars, than to the perspicacity of Government.' No Governor-General that we ever remember has been so addressed by his subordinates, and we cannot help expressing our admiration at the bold and uncompromising manner in which Mr. Grey and Sir Henry Durand convey views to the Governor-General on a subject on which he was not only wrong, but in regard to which by persisting in its prosecution placed the Imperial Government in a humiliating and almost degrading position. Sir John receives these keen reproofs in silence, orders that the papers be forwarded to the Secretary of State as soon as possible, and reserves to himself the right of replying to Mr. Grey's and Colonel Durand's Minutes. We hope he will not delay long before doing so, as we confess to a curiosity to see the reply of a Governor-General to such biting remarks."

The taluqdars never questioned the *motives* of the Governor-General in instituting the inquiry. In the loyal Address which they presented to him in November 1867, they said: "We respect your Excellency's benevolent designs with regard to the lasting welfare of our tenants, and we take this opportunity to assure your Excellency that we look upon them as members of our own families, and we believe that our interests, closely bound with those of our tenants, form the best safeguard of harmony and mutual good-will."

CHAPTER VI.

OUDH LEGISLATION.

In October 1866, a Bill was introduced into the Legislativ Council of the Governor-General, called the "Oudh Sub-Settlement Bill." This was afterwards known as the "Oudh Sub-Settlement Act, 1866." The Act is very short. It contains only three sections, but it defined and determined the most important interests. The first section contains the following pregnant words:—

Oudh Sub-Settlement Act.

"The rules for determining the conditions under which persons possessed of subordinate rights of property in taluqas in the territories subject to the administration of the Chief Commissioner of Oudh, shall be entitled to obtain a sub-settlement of lands, villages or subdivisions thereof, which they held under taluqdars on or before the 13th day of February 1856, and for determining the amounts payable to the taluqdars by such subordinate proprietors, which rules were made by the said Chief Commissioner, sanctioned by the Governor-General of India in Council, and published in the *Gazette of India* for September 1st, 1866, are hereby declared to have the force of law."

In introducing the Bill, Mr. Muir said: "The measures being of local application, and sufficiently known and approved by all who were likely to give any opinion on the subject, being, moreover, the result of a kind of compromise which Government had ratified, it was of importance that the Bill should be introduced and passed at once, and that the faith of Government should thus be maintained by placing the rules beyond the doubt of any want of legal validity." "It is of the first consequence," he added, "to maintain the faith of Government inviolate."

It was objected that the Bill related to only one part of the arrangements lately concluded, and if the rules for sub-proprietary rights were passed into law, so also should that portion of the rules which related to cultivating rights. The Governor-General said in reply that, with respect to the rights of occupying tenants, he firmly believed that the taluqdars would act in good faith towards the ryots, and that if any difficulty should arise, legislation might then be resorted to. "The great argument," he said, "in favor of the taluqdars was that, although they had always denied the existence of rights of occupancy in Oudh, and though their sunuds were silent as to such rights, they were willing to grant certain privileges to the class of ancient proprietors of the soil who, although they had lost all proprietary right, still occupied as cultivators land in their ancestral villages. The ready assent which the taluqdars had given to the proposed measures as to the sub-settlement also justified the expectation that they could carry out to its entirety the scheme now proposed to be legalized."

The rules which related to the second part of the arrangements, *viz.*, the rights of a certain class of occupying tenants, have been also passed into law. The law which determines the occupancy rights of the descendants of former proprietors is known as the Oudh Rent Act, XIX of 1868. By this Act the descendants of certain persons who were in proprietary possession of the village in which the lands are situated, within the thirty years next preceding the annexation of the Province, enjoy certain substantial privileges. These persons possess "a heritable, but not a transferable, right of occupancy." The tenant with a right of occupancy holds on certain favorable terms, which are 12½ per cent., or two annas in the rupee, less than the terms of rent prevailing in adjacent fields held by ordinary tenants, and, as his designation implies, he is not liable to ejectment at the will of the landlord. His right, though hereditary, is not transferable.

The Oudh Rent Act.

Under the Oudh law, no mere length of possession can create any right in favor of a tenant-at-will or squatter. If a present tenant's ancestors never enjoyed a proprietary right in the village, he is nothing more than a tenant-at-will.

In no case can the Courts interfere between landlord and

tenant to determine the amount of rent to be demanded from an ordinary cultivator. But if any tenant construct works of permanent utility, such as masonry wells, watercourses, or the like, he cannot be ousted, nor can his rent be raised, until he has received compensation for his outlay on the improvements.

The rules regarding sub-settlement and other subordinate rights of property, to which Act XXVI of 1866 gave the force of law, provided for the great majority of the cases affecting the relative positions of the taluqdars and of the under-proprietors. There were certain "hard cases," however, which were not touched by that Act. Cases occurred in which, without intention whatever of conferring a reward, villages were for some reason or other summarily settled, in the confusion of the times, with a taluqdar, and were inserted accordingly in his sunud, which were not included in his taluqa before Annexation. In these cases the taluqdar, in virtue of the sunuds conferred upon him, was the sole proprietor, and the former proprietor was deprived of all his rights. If the application of a remedy for the hardships which the former proprietors suffered in such cases as these involved any infringement of the engagements entered into by the British Government, or any interference with the rights which had been bestowed upon the taluqdars, nothing could now be done. These hardships must be accepted as unavoidable consequences of the revolution which swept over the country in 1857-58. But there was no necessity of the kind. In nearly all the cases in which there was even a shadow of injustice resulting from the taluqdari settlement in Oudh, not only were the taluqdars willing that a remedy should be applied, but were ready to lend their cordial co-operation which could reasonably be expected from them, provided that nothing was done to affect the position which they held under their sunuds. While questions like those of sub-settlement and of rights of occupancy were pending,—questions which the taluqdars naturally believed to be of vital importance to their interests,—it was hardly to be expected that they would be inclined to look favourably upon measures which involved an admission on their part that the strict terms ought, in some cases, to be modified. As soon as

"Hard cases."

these important questions of sub-settlement and tenant-rights were disposed of to the satisfaction of all parties, there was every disposition on the part of the taluqdars generally to consider, in a liberal spirit, what steps could be taken for the removal of the hardships of which complaint had been made. The taluqdars of their own accord submitted propositions which appeared to the Chief Commissioner to be "very liberal," when it was considered that the persons in whose favor they were made had no legal right whatever to anything at all, and that they could now obtain nothing except by the voluntary concessions of the taluqdars. "If the propositions," said Sir John Strachey (February 8, 1867), "that have now been made be carried out in a liberal spirit, we shall be able to say at least this much, that the former proprietors of the land, whose rights were swept away by the measures of our Government in 1858, have been replaced, as a general rule, in a position scarcely inferior to that which they held before the annexation of the Province," and more than this could not be expected by the dispossessed proprietor, or most warm advocate of their rights. Had it not been for the voluntary concessions made so liberally and generously by the taluqdars, the *former* proprietors could never have regained any portion whatever of their alleged rights.

The taluqdars were extremely anxious to repair any wrong that might have been unintentionally done. They were fully aware that their cause would not suffer; on the contrary, would be greatly strengthened by acknowledging the rights of those who believed, rightly or wrongly, that they were "injured" by the taluqdari settlement. The Chief Commissioner, in submitting the proposals made by the taluqdars to the Governor-General, hoped that His Excellency would be of opinion "that these propositions reflect credit upon the taluqdars of this province, and in particular upon Maharajah Maun Singh, to whose exertions the results that have been obtained are mainly due." "These propositions show," he added, "that the taluqdars are themselves quite alive to the fact that their position must be materially improved and strengthened by the removal of causes" which might in the least cause any dissatisfaction to the Government. Strong in the justice of their cause, they could afford to be liberal, and whatever might be said by captious critics of the taluqdari settlement, it could never be said of the taluqdars, that standing "on the letter of their sunuds," they ever shrank from doing *justice* to those who demanded it from them There can be no question whatever that "the more consonant with justice the taluqdari settlement can be made, the more stable will it become," and the taluqdars have taken every opportunity to show that the policy inaugurated by Lord Canning in Oudh is productive of the best results The Governor-General approved of the arrangements proposed by the taluqdars to remove the "hardships" complained of, and assured them that the concessions made were very "creditable" to them.

Sir Stafford Northcote's review of the final settlement of the "Occupancy" question :

The Secretary of State, Sir Stafford Northcote, in reviewing the correspondence of the India Government relating to the final settlement of the important subject of occupancy rights, wrote to the Governor-General (October 29, 1866):—"I learn with much pleasure that a question so long agitated has now been settled, in a manner which appears to be in every respect satisfactory, alike to your Excellency's Government and to the taluqdars I have been much gratified at observing the high terms of commendation in which you speak of the conduct of the officers at the head of the Administration in Oudh, and of the taluqdars themselves, through whose joint instrumentality this arrangement has been concluded; and I trust that the result of the measure will be such as to secure the continuance of confidence and good-will among all classes of the agricultural community in that important province."

I will not multiply these extracts. As a final word, however, on the subject of occupancy rights, I would quote the following from a speech of Lord Macaulay :—

"'I have a right to do what I will with my own.' There would be an end of property if you were to interdict a landlord from ejecting a tenant. . . . . The principle of the right of property is, that a man is not only to be allowed to dispose of his wealth rationally and usefully, but to be allowed . . . . to let, or refuse to let, his land according to his own pleasure, without giving any reason, or asking any body's leave."—(Lord Macaulay's Works, Vol. VIII, p. 147.)

The Conclusion.

All's well that ends well. The province, after being agitated for so many years by these vexed questions, had at last a fair prospect of enjoying long and continued peace. Even the stanch advocates of tenant-rights, "the disciples of the old revenue vision-seers," frankly admitted that the conduct of the taluqdars in the late controversy was most praiseworthy, and that the taluqdars did not on any occasion try to take undue advantage of their position. Even pre-existing prejudices, pet-theories, and foregone conclusions, had to give way, and the taluqdari policy was vindicated. The taluqdars, who were most anxious about the result of the agitation that was going on, rejoiced to find that their rights were confirmed, and that their dignity and position, as contemplated by Lord Canning's Government, were maintained. Confident in the goodness of their cause and their ultimate victory whenever assailed, they can afford to smile when they are calumniated by the disciples of the Thomasonian School. It is a common saying that vituperation is indulged in when argument fails us. It is not easy for any person to give up ideas which he has cherished for a long time. "To be the slave of an idea is more or less the fate of individuals and communities. It was decapitation in China to doubt that the emperor was the brother of the sun and the moon; it was political death in America to doubt that all nations would receive the law from Washington, annex themselves to its mild realms, and bow to its easy yoke;" and it was political excommunication among a sect of rulers in the North-West to doubt that the socialistic village system was indigenous to the land. The terrible civil war which desolated China and America, and the bloody storm which swept over Hindustan, incontrovertibly demonstrated the utter futility of these exploded theories. Nevertheless the advocates of these effete systems never recede from their error. They walk, says the *Times*, as in a trance, political somnambulists bound by their own spell, and serving a phantom of their own creation. The opinion of Lord Palmerston is surely entitled to the highest respect. Denouncing the communistic system, he said that "it was totally at variance with the whole fabric of a civil organization, to which we attach so much value, and upon which the interest and prosperity of the country depend. Let the owner and the tenant settle their own affairs." The North-West revenue-seers would continually interfere between the landlord and his tenants, and arrest the healthy progress of the country. In vain are they told that Government intervention in such matters, instead of promoting agricultural prosperity, only tends to cause agricultural deterioration, and instead of securing the well-being of tenants, creates grounds of oppression, by disturbing harmony and producing ill-will among them. They are deaf to these arguments, and would continually harp upon the "miseries" and the "wretched state" of the Indian cultivators, which assuredly do exist nowhere except in their morbid imagination. We hear them say that the Oudh cultivators are "underfed, and generally underclothed. Had they been underfed, surely they would not have been such robust men as they are, and the population of Oudh would not have increased so rapidly as it has within the last ten years. As to their being underclothed, it is enough to say that they do not require a very large wardrobe. Surely they do not need laced caps and *kinkhab chogas* when they work in the fields. The hot climate of India, one would think, demands but a slender *wardrobe* for the tillers of the soil. This ridiculous statement about the Oudh cultivators being "underclothed," reminds us of the rather amusing story told of Francis, the Junius of Macaulay, the firebrand of Hastings' Council, who, when he landed in Calcutta, seeing the natives walking barefooted, exclaimed that no stronger proof was required of the tyrranous rule of Hastings than the fact that the poor natives walked "barefooted." Why does not the Government supply them with shoes? The tenants of Oudh are as well off as they are expected to be. The very fact of their digging 6,476 common wells, and 913 masonry wells, within four years (1861—1864), indisputably shows that they have larger resources than "a pair of lean little oxen, half-a-dozen pots and pans, a few rude agricultural implements, and a little silver jewellery." We also read that the cultivators dug several thousand wells in the late drought. What stronger proof is required, we wonder, of the cultivators being in a prosperous condition than the fact of their being able to dig expensive wells to irrigate their lands. Say what you may, they are much better off than tenants of other provinces.*

The passionate advocates of tenant-rights speak in enthusiastic terms of *grande* and *petite culture,* of the metayer system, and the *laisser-faire* principle, and evidently wish to draw an analogy between these systems and the indigenous revenue systems of Oudh. If, instead of trying to find a fancied resemblance between two opposite systems, they would devote their energies to ameliorate the condition of the people by administering the existing laws with justice and equity, they would earn the lasting gratitude of the country, and enjoy the luxury of performing their duties, and doing good to the people. We are asked, "Are the cultivators to rise above their present condition?" The answer to this question is not difficult to find. We have but one answer to give to the questions—"How are the labouring classes to better their condition? How are they to rise and shake off their dependence? Educate and enlighten them, and they will attain a position as happy and honorable as that of their more fortunate countrymen. Their welfare entirely depends on their mental cultivation. Refined notions of property and social position are the results of education. The diffusion of useful knowledge among the masses, will awaken public spirit and rouse thought and reflection in the more intelligent. The energetic and the enter-

* "The Lieutenant-Governor has put on record, from time to time, in former reviews, and now at greater length in this, all the evidence at his command on the condition of the tenantry in Oudh. It is gratifying to him, as it must be to all, to have in this evidence the assurance that this condition is on the whole steadily improving. There are exceptions, but, as more than one officer has remarked, they are exceptions and not the rule. . . . . The tenantry are less interfered with in their little farms, and they receive in seasons of bad harvests (from men of large possessions) help in the foregoing of rents, which is impossible to the straitened owners of small estates. The feudal attachments of landlord and tenant are not yet dead in the ancient baronies of Oudh, and this review itself contains some noble examples of generous and active help in time of difficulty by the Rajput chiefs to their tenantry."—(Revenue Report, 1881, p. 101.)

prising, feeling the inferiority of their position, will apply themselves to business, and, in due time, earn the rewards of their industry. Thus will the deserving raise themselves to a level with the aristocracy. By aristocracy, we do not mean a body the members of which are to roll in wealth, to despise all manly occupations, and, in ignorance of the graces of literature and the truths of science, to pass their time in idleness and dissipation. We have as great an aversion to such useless men as other nations have. The sooner so unproductive a class is swept away, the better. We speak of the aristocracy of intellect, of knowledge, and of energy conjoined with wealth. It is only by possessing these attributes that the native nobility could be of any use to themselves or to their country. These are the necessary conditions of their existence; and when an individual of the higher ranks is wanting in them, he, in obedience to the laws of nature, *falls,* to make room for another more deserving. The former sinks to his proper level, while the other rises, and taking upon himself the duties and responsibilities of his predecessor, enjoys all the advantages of the superior position he has reached. We could cite numerous instances among our fellow-subjects in Bengal, of individuals who have risen from a humble sphere to rank and affluence, even prior to the introduction of refined notions about tenant-rights, and the metayer system and the *laisser-faire* principle. In fact, greater stability is imparted to the aristocracy by the infusion of these new elements. This augments its strength, sustains its vigor, and diminishes the number of its adversaries. Thus, without destroying the fundamental principles of society and the rights of property, and without encroaching on the legitimate field of the hopes and aspirations of the working classes, an equilibrium will be maintained. It is not by ignoring the liberty of action and independence of thought of the higher orders that we can attain the desired result. Our legislators forget the lessons of history, when they pursue this erroneous course. Until the rule indicated above be adopted, do what you will to elevate the lower orders, your exertions, however well-meant, will fail.

The taluqdars, as we have said, possess the full right of property in their estates, and their titles rest on a firm basis.

Protected by their sunuds and by Act I of 1869, the title of a taluqdar is perfectly unassailable. By the same Act too the taluqdar has been freed from the provisions of the ordinary Hindu Sastras and Mahomedan Shar'a, and out of the two hundred and fifty-six taluqdars, a large number have adopted the law of primogeniture. Subject to certain provisions, every taluqdar can bequeath by will the whole or any portion of his estate.

Sir John Strachey, in moving (11th January 1869) that the Report of the Select Committee on the Bill to define the rights of taluqdars and others in certain estates in Oudh be taken into consideration, said :—" After the recapture of Lucknow in March 1858, Lord Canning issued his Proclamation under which the whole of the land in Oudh was confiscated to the British Government. This Proclamation became the means of redressing the injustice which was undoubtedly done to the taluqdars at the first occupation of the province. It gave to Sir Robert Montgomery the power of making his arrangements for the pacification of Oudh, unfettered by anything previously done; and this Proclamation, which was originally intended as a sentence of punishment and confiscation against the taluqdars, became ultimately, in the hands of Sir Robert Montgomery, the means of enlisting them on the side of the British Government. The political arrangements then entered into by Sir Robert Montgomery formed the basis of the subsequent policy of Lord Canning; and in October 1859, Lord Canning issued the well-known orders on which the rights of the taluqdars now depend. By these orders the taluqdars were not only confirmed in the possession of everything they held at the Annexation of Oudh, 1856, but new rights of a valuable nature were also conferred on them.

Act I, 1869.

" The taluqdar, who holds a sunud from the Government, has strictly a personal and exclusive right to the property in his estate; the taluqdar, instead of holding his estate, as formerly, under the obligations of the Hindu and Mahomedan law, according to which his power of alienation by sale or gift beyond his lifetime was very limited, now possesses the absolute power of disposing of his estates as he likes. There was much difference of opinion between Sir Charles Wingfield and Lord Canning in regard to the conditions under which the taluqdars ought to hold their estates. Lord Canning would not consent to limit the absolute power over his estate which had been guaranteed to every taluqdar in Oudh, and was convinced that the existence of such a power was just as essential to the prosperity of the province and to the maintenance of a landed aristocracy on a sound footing as the extension of the rule of primogeniture in cases of intestacy. Lord Canning thus refused to admit the validity of the objections of Sir Charles Wingfield, and the taluqdars were distinctly told that they would possess absolute power in disposing of their estates. Now I, for my part, entirely agree in the remarks made by the Hon'ble Sir Henry Durand in the debate on the introduction of this Bill, to the effect that no limitation can now properly be put on the absolute rights conferred on the taluqdars of Oudh by Lord Canning, unless with the full consent of the taluqdars themselves.

"When this Bill came before the Council, the Hon'ble Sir Henry Durand expressed a wish that we had as a Member of this Council a representative of the taluqdars of Oudh, who would be able to speak with authority on their behalf. Fortunately that wish of Sir Henry Durand has lately been fulfilled; and we have now as a Member of this Council my friend the Hon'ble Sir Digbijay Singh, the Maharaja of Bulrampore, who is well known not only to the Council, but I may say to the whole country, as the most eminent representative of all the taluqdars of Oudh. I think, therefore, that I need not say much as to the real wishes of the taluqdars themselves in regard to this Bill, because Sir Digbijay Singh can speak on such a point with infinitely greater authority than I can speak myself."

The Hon'ble Maharaja Sir Digbijay Singh spoke to the following effect:—"The popular and useful rules and regulations passed by His Excellency the late Lord Canning and brought into action by Sir Charles Wingfield, together with the sunuds, imbued the minds of the taluqdars and the tenantry of Oudh with a feeling of peace and security, and the prosperity which resulted needs no comment. Similarly, when, during the course of the regular settlement of the different taluqdars, this feeling was, in a measure, disturbed by the institution of a vast number of cases by the near kinsmen, the sub-proprietors and the cultivators of the soil, all desirous of having their rights justly defined, the Hon'ble Mr. Strachey, Mr. Davies, and Colonel Barrow spared no trouble in preparing, according to your Excellency's suggestions, and with the concurrence and assistance of the taluqdars, the Bill now under your Excellency's consideration. This, in my humble opinion and in that of the taluqdars generally, is fully calculated to establish, with greater precision and clearness, our rights over our estates, and by setting aside all doubt and cause of dispute, to place us in more substantial security. Being thus blessed, I beg herewith to tender to your Excellency my warmest thanks on behalf of the whole community, who will for ever pray to the Almighty for your Excellency's long life and daily increasing prosperity."

The Hon'ble Sir George Couper, who was then in the Council, said :—

"The late Lord Canning gave the taluqdars of Oudh the absolute right of alienation in their estates,—that is he gave them the right to alienate their estates by gift or will or sale, or in whatever manner they pleased, and at whatever time they pleased. Sir Charles Wingfield, who was then Chief Commissioner of Oudh, and who certainly could not be accused of any undue bias against the taluqdars, represented to Lord Canning that he proposed to give them more than was allowed either by the Mahomedan or by the Hindu law, and more than was enjoyed by any other landholders in any other part of India. In spite, however, of Sir Charles Wingfield's remonstrances, repeated over and over again in language as strong as an officer in the position of a Chief Commissioner could venture to use when addressing a Viceroy, Lord Canning adhered to his original determination, and the letters to the Chief Commissioner, in which he invested the taluqdars with the right to alienate their estates how and when they would, were believed, under the Indian Council's Acts, to have the force of law, although, as pointed out by his Hon'ble friend the Mover, the highest legal authority thought it not impossible that the Judicial Committee of Her Majesty's Privy Council might be of a different opinion.

"Now this Bill, while confirming the taluqdars in the rights of alienation vested in them by Lord Canning, imposed certain restrictions on the exercise of those rights. At present a taluqdar, actuated by the freak of the moment, or actuated by fright of the moment, as the case might be, could disinherit his whole family in favor of a clever dancing-girl, or of a designing priest. The power of acting in this manner would not be taken from him; but before doing so, he would have to observe certain formalities regarding which it was unnecessary for him (Sir George Couper) to enter into fully, seeing that they had been touched upon by his Hon'ble friend the Mover, and must be apparent to everyone who had read through the sections of the Bill. It seemed to him that nothing could be more just and equitable in themselves than these restrictions on an arbitrary power to alienate. Still, however, they were restrictions, and as such, under ordinary circumstances, he would oppose them. For, he submitted, any restriction by the Legislature, under ordinary circumstances, on a promise formally and deliberately made by a Viceroy ten years previously, whether that promise in itself was right, or whether it was wrong, could not but be strongly deprecated.

"For it was with the view to pacification after the Mutiny that Lord Canning conferred this right to alienate on the taluqdars of Oudh. At the same time he conferred certain other privileges, notably the right of adoption, on the chiefs of Central India and other feudatories; and if those chiefs, under ordinary circumstances, were to see the right so bestowed on the taluqdars of Oudh restricted in its operation ten years afterwards by legislative enactment, it stood to reason that they and everybody else would lose all confidence in the integrity of Lord Canning's promises, and would naturally regard them as so much waste paper. Moreover, in the event of troublous times recurring, the best inducement which a Viceroy would have to offer influential natives to espouse our cause would be the prospect of preferment or reward in land in the shape of a jagir or otherwise; and this, which, as far as he knew, was the most powerful instrument, if it would not indeed be the only instrument in the hands of a Viceroy, under such circumstances as happened in 1857, would be rendered of no avail if it once got abroad, that the solemn and deliberate promise of a Viceroy was liable to be subjected to restrictions, at a subsequent period, by an Act of this Council, or any other authority.

"Sir George Couper would ask His Excellency, who was in the most trying position of them all in 1857—he would ask His Excellency he said—to conceive a repetition of 1857, without the God-send of the China contingent, and with the route through Egypt stopped, and the Viceroy, in his desperate need, offering, say, Sindiah, one or more districts in the Province of Bandelkand, or Holkar the restoration of one or more of his Ceded Districts. He did not mean for a moment to say that it would be right to adopt such an extreme measure, still less that it would be necessary. That of course would depend upon the exigency of the circumstances. But if the Viceroy did take such a step, what would his feelings be?—what would the feelings of every other Englishman be?—if either of those feudatories were to reply that the promise would suffice to induce him to cast in his lot with us if it could only be trusted; but, as he had no security that the Legislature would not at some future date impose restrictions on the grant, he preferred to try his fortunes elsewhere,—that is, he preferred to see whether he could not get all that the Viceroy offered, and perhaps more besides, by ranging himself on the side of our enemies.

"It was, therefore, only under the most special and exceptional circumstances that Sir George Couper would vote for the passing of this Bill. Such circumstances, however, did really exist in this instance. They had been stated by his Hon'ble friend the Mover, they had been confirmed by his Hon'ble friend the Maharajah of Bulrampore, and might be summed up in the fact that, in consideration of the benefits which they will otherwise derive from the Bill, the taluqdars of Oudh have formally expressed their wish and desire that the restrictions which it imposes on their original right to alienate may be made.

"This seemed to him (Sir George Couper) sufficient to satisfy the most jealous guardian of our national faith as represented by the promises of a former Viceroy. For the chiefs of Central India will know that, unless they themselves request that restrictions may be imposed on their right of adoption, Lord Canning's promises to them in that regard will be respected. Nor will any other past or future recipient of a Viceregal gift or privilege be disposed to distrust its validity, if he knows that he can only be restricted in its exercise with his own free will and consent.

"Sir George Couper had ventured to trespass at this length on the patience of the Council for two reasons: *First*, because, bearing in mind the fact that the Bill will impose restrictions on the right to alienate bestowed by Lord Canning, and hitherto enjoyed by the taluqdars, he thought it highly desirable that the public in general and the native community in particular should fully and thoroughly understand that the Bill had been introduced and would be passed, if it were passed, with the full consent and approbation of those whose interests were most immediately affected. *Secondly*, because he thought His Excellency and the Hon'ble Members might perhaps like to hear from the lips of a man who was at Sir Charles Wingfield's right hand during his advocacy of the cause of the taluqdars in 1864 and in 1865, and who might, therefore, fairly claim to have their interests at heart, that he believed the provisions of this Bill would be conducive to those interests in the fullest and the truest meaning of the words, so much so that, unless it were passed, the original object which Lord Canning declared himself to have in view, the creation of a powerful landed aristocracy in Oudh, would, in the course of a generation, be completely defeated."

The Governor-General said:

"The Hon'ble Sir Digbijay Singh has expressed his satisfaction at the prospect of the Bill before the Council being passed to-day; I am also glad to be able to participate in that satisfaction. The Bill has been drawn with the view of giving the taluqdars of Oudh as complete rights as they wished over their estates, and, I may venture to say, as full powers as can reasonably be desired. I think with the Hon'ble Mr. Strachey that the limitations proposed on the power of alienating estates are wise and judicious. I can only desire further to add, that I trust that the policy, which, I hope, will this day receive the sanction of the Council, will be so worked by the taluqdars and their descendants that we never shall have cause to regret that policy. It is in the hands of the taluqdars themselves to make their privileges a blessing or a misfortune to their relatives, to the subordinate proprietor, and to the cultivators of the soil; and I trust that they and their descendants will so discharge the duties which are bound up with their rights that the British Government will be satisfied that the policy which is now being declared is sound." The Governor-General then proposed that a measure should be introduced into the Council which should have for its object to relieve those taluqdars "who were in circumstances of difficulty, partly owing to circumstances which occurred during the Mutiny." "It is hard for any man," as the Governor-General justly said, "placed in the position of a taluqdar to be just and generous when he has difficulties in his own home." "The measure I propose," added the Governor-General, "appears to me to be justified by sound policy, and I trust it will also have the effect of showing the taluqdars of Oudh that the British Government really desires that they should be maintained in prosperity in their present position."

The Hon'ble Major-General Sir Henry Durand said, that the proposal made by the Governor-General in favor of embarrassed taluqdars was sure to meet with a favorable reception and consideration by the Council. As for himself, there was every disposition on his part to entertain favorably a well-considered measure of the kind indicated, "because I feel," he said, "that the conduct of the taluqdars has throughourt, both in the consideration of the previous Oudh Bill and of the present Bill, been, for many reasons, which I shall not enter upon, really admirable."

At the conclusion of the proceedings, Sir John Strachey paid a graceful tribute to the Governor-General:—"Sir, I will not say anything more than that I think it a cause of great satisfaction that this Bill should be passed into law before your Excellency's departure. The last important public act of Lord Canning was the bringing in of a Bill to give the force of law to the arrangements which he had made in Oudh. Similarly, one of the last public acts of your Excellency will be to give your Excellency's assent to the Bill, the avowed object of which is to carry out and confirm the policy of Lord Canning, and which has been received by the taluqdars as the complete fulfilment of the engagements entered into by the British Government. I venture to assert, that by the passing of this Bill your Excellency will be remembered hereafter as one of the greatest and truest of the benefactors of the taluqdars of Oudh."

The Bill then became law, and is now known as Act I of 1869.

The Governor-General said above, that it was in the hands of the taluqdars themselves to make their privileges a blessing or a misfortune to the subordinate proprietors and to the cultivators of the soil. The taluqdars, as is well known, have discharged the duties which are bound up with their rights in such a just and equitable manner as to give universal satisfaction. If proof were wanting, we would, in support of our statement, point to the contentment of the sub-proprietors, who are always treated with kindness and consideration, and to the general prosperity of the Oudh tenantry. Speaking of the management of some of the taluqdari estates in Oudh, His Honor the Lieutenant-Governor said (Administration Report, p. 32, 1880):—"Nearly 90 per cent. of the true rental of the year was collected, and the total rent collections were equal to 99¾ per cent. of a full year's rental. These results are highly satisfactory, indicating, as they do, the general prosperity of the tenantry, whose circumstances may be taken as fairly representing those of the agricultural classes generally throughout the province." It is thus evident from the above facts and figures that even on economical grounds the taluqdari policy is perfectly sound.

The Oudh Land-Revenue Act.

The Oudh Land Revenue Act was passed in October 1876. It is known as Act XVII of 1876. Its object is to consolidate and define the law regulating the settlement and collection of land-revenue in Oudh. It is in fact a collection of rules which were previously contained in a mass of old Regulations, Acts, and Orders. There is some little new matter; but, speaking broadly, the Act is simply a codification of the previously existing law. This law is a corollary of the action initiated to define the general law of the province, and it afforded an opportunity of discarding many obsolete provisions, of simplifying the law, and of introducing amendments of benefit to the general body of the landowners. The Bill, when it was in Council, created a feeling of uneasiness among the taluqdars. They thought they were going to be deprived of some of their valued rights and privileges. "That the landowners," said the Chief Commissioner (*Oudh Government Gazette, January* 11, 1873), "have received it in the light of a beneficial enactment, it would be simply untrue to assert. As a body, unfamiliar with the misty laws reproduced in this new form, and content with a revenue administration which has been rarely obliged to resort to coercive measures of any severity, they have been no doubt startled by the naked statement of the law under which they live. This result was scarcely anticipated, and it is in some respects unfortunate, but it is of importance that the people should know the law to which they are subject, and it is an advantage that they should have been given a distinct opportunity of expressing their opinion upon it."

The Committee of the British Indian Association of Oudh, in respectfully representing their objections to the Bill in the form in which it was introduced into the Council, said :—

"The Committee never objected to the 'laws and regulations' regarding the collection and assessment of the land-revenue, 'which are already in force' in the province. They objected only to the introduction into the province of those *new laws*, rules, and regulations which would militate against the policy of Lord Canning and affect the rights solemnly guaranteed to the taluqdars by Her Majesty's Government. The taluqdars were not 'startled by the naked statement of the law under which they live,' but they were startled by those provisions in the Bill which would overbear their rights and degrade them in the eyes of the world. The taluqdars need hardly say that their honor is dearer to them than even the loss of their lives or earthly possessions . . . . The taluqdars wish to live in peace with the inferior holders and the ryots It is for their sake, as well as their own, that the taluqdars earnestly wish that the disputes and differences, which have unsettled the minds of all classes of the community, may soon be put an end to. In 1866, Sir John Strachey 'confidently hoped to see a complete and immediate termination to all the unfortunate dissensions and discussions by which, for so long a period, the Province of Oudh had been distracted.' Six more years have passed away, and that 'termination' has not yet been reached.

"The taluqdars have never been allowed to enjoy rest and to devote their attention to the improvement of their estates and the advancement of their tenants. One measure after another has been introduced into Oudh to disturb their feeling of security. The Secretary of State spoke in 1860 of identifying the fixing of the (taluqdari) tenures with the stability of the British Government under which they are held; and the taluqdars often think with great delight on those ever memorable words of Lord Canning, with which he assured the taluqdars in open Durbar, that the rights and dignity of the taluqdars would be upheld by every representative of the Queen, and that 'no man shall ever disturb them.'

"The taluqdars do not at all desire to injure the rights of others. All that they wish is to enjoy their own rights in peace."

Material modifications, which the expressions of the opinion of the taluqdars suggested, were made in the Bill, and the feeling of uneasiness which they felt subsided.

The Hon'ble Mr. Inglis, in moving that the final Report of the Select Committee on the Bill to consolidate and define the law relating to land-revenue in Oudh be taken into consideration, acknowledged, in handsome terms, "the great assistance which the Select Committee received from the taluqdars of Oudh, who had from the first taken a very active and intelligent interest in the Bill." "I wish," he said, "to take advantage of this opportunity to express, as Officiating Chief Commissioner of Oudh, my sense of the fairness and liberality that have been shown by the taluqdars as a body in the discussion and settlement of the many important questions affecting their rights and interests that have been raised while this Bill has been before the Select Committee. I refer especially to my friend the

Maharajah of Bulrampore, who is now a Member of the Council; to Raja Amir Hussen Khan, who is the Vice-President of the Taluqdars' Association; and also to the other taluqdars who have come up to Simla to be present at the final discussion on it. I have now, my Lord, to move that the final Report of the Select Committee on the Bill be taken into consideration."

The Hon'ble the Maharajah of Bulrampore, speaking in Hindustani, said that the Oudh Land-Revenue Bill and the Oudh Laws Bill had been under consideration for the last four years. During this interval all those taluqdars and others whom the provisions of this Bill concerned were given the opportunity to express their opinion. Consequently, every section of these Bills was properly discussed and thoroughly considered, and the several points were thoroughly determined by the Select Committee. In his opinion the legislation of these Bills was in reality an important one, for by their introduction many doubts had been removed. It was, therefore, his desire that the Bills might be passed by the Council.

The motion was put and agreed to.

The Hon'ble Mr. Inglis also moved that the Bill as amended be passed.

His Excellency the President said:—

"Before I put the question which has been moved by the Hon'ble Mr. Inglis, that the Bill be passed, I wish to say a very few words regarding the subject of this Bill. It is not in my power to add anything, nor is it necessary that I should attempt to add anything in the way of explanation to the much that has been already written and spoken, and more especially to what we have heard to-day from the Hon'ble Member, who moved that the Bill do now pass, respecting the details of this important measure, the circumstances which have rendered it necessary, or the numerous objects it is intended to effect. But the probable result of the motion, with which I shall conclude these remarks, is one upon which I desire to offer the sincere congratulations and grateful acknowledgments of the Government of India,—in the first place, to those able and experienced administrators Sir George Couper and Mr. Inglis, as also to the Judicial Commissioner in Oudh, Mr. Currie, who, by their valuable advice and energetic assistance, have enabled the Committee to bring this Bill to, what we hope and believe, a satisfactory conclusion; and, in the next place, I wish to offer similar and no less cordial acknowledgments to the Maharajah of Bulrampore, and to those influential native noblemen and gentlemen of Oudh whose intelligent co-operation and unprejudiced criticism have so greatly aided the Government of India in its endeavour to reconcile the reasonable interests of the taluqdars, with that degree of security which the State in its supreme capacity, as the impartial guardian of all classes and interests, is bound to provide, not only for the collection of its own revenue, but also for the rights of subordinate holders and the adequate protection of the actual cultivator of the soil.

"It is with especial satisfaction that I notice that our deliberations to-day have taken place in the presence of some of those gentlemen who so worthily represent the intelligence and loyalty of the taluqdars of Oudh; because I am thereby publicly afforded the opportunity of vindicating, in their hearing, the character of this Government from a very serious accusation, which has been publicly preferred against it by a writer of considerable eminence and authority. In a recent work by him upon the Primitive forms of property, M. Evile de Laveleye, the distinguished Belgian Publicist, has recorded and criticized the course of Indian legislation in reference to land-tenures in Oudh. Now no doubt this subject is a very complicated and difficult one, but I fear it cannot be said that M. de Laveleye has treated it with his usual care and candour; indeed, statements on the subject appear to me to have been made under a total misconception, not only of the principles, but also of the plainest facts of our Indian land legislation. Those statements, however, have so special a reference to the questions with which this Bill is concerned, that before I refer to them more particularly in detail, it may, perhaps, be convenient to revert for a moment to the origin and object of the measure now before us:

"The primary object of the Bill is, as we have heard from my Hon'ble friend Mr. Inglis, to clarify the laws relating to land-revenue in Oudh, which have been obscured and confused by section 25 of the Indian Council's Act. That section declares to be law a great number of merely executive orders and regulations which were never intended to be law at all. Mr. Hobhouse gave us the other day the number of enactments which have been more or less applied in Oudh, subject to indefinite qualification by the executive order of February 1856; and if I rightly recollect, it was no less than 247. I gathered from this lucid analysis of the state of the law in Oudh that it consisted, *firstly*, of the spirit of the Bengal Regulations modified by custom; *secondly*, of a few Acts of Council having special application to Oudh; and, *thirdly*, of this mass of executive orders to which I have referred; and of which, I believe, it was said by a very eminent former member of this Council (Sir Henry S. Maine), that he could rarely read one of them without being in doubt whether it was intended to convey a sarcasm or to lay down a rule. Well, the present system of land-revenue in Oudh, which this Bill, when passed, will materially modify, and we trust will greatly improve, was based on the Punjab system, as that system existed in what I suppose I may call the pre-scientific era,—that is to say, before it had been codified by Mr. FitzJames Stephen and Mr. Egerton, and the Bill now before us was, I believe, when first introduced, drawn upon the lines of the Punjab Act, XXXIII of 1871.

"Since then, I need not say it has been copiously recast in general accordance with the principles of the North-Western Provinces Act, XIX of 1873. Now, it is quite unnecessary for me to follow the Bill through all its previous stages, to the final and definite form in which I hope to pass it to-day.

"The history of the Bill has been very ably sketched by the Hon'ble Members, who not only on this, but on former occasions, have spoken on the subject of it; and, in listening to the exceedingly interesting account they have given us of the progress of this measure, I have often been reminded of a very curious and extraordinary statement (a statement almost as extraordinary as that of M. de Laveleye) by an old Greek writer, who seriously affirms it to be a fact in natural history, that the eagle habitually lays three eggs, sits upon two, and hatches only one. Now, however untrustworthy that statement may be in regard to the natural history of eagles, I think it is, at least, more or less applicable to the natural history of the legislative incubations and productions of a Government, which, like this, of India, has to legislate with careful reference to the most complete, the most curious, and the most delicate diversities and varieties in the fundamental social facts of the numerous dissimilar communities whose rights and interests are committed to its charge. In fact, the Indian Legislature, in reference to subjects like the present, is obliged to deal with its Bills much in the same way as the eagle has been said to deal with her eggs,—that is to say, the Bills finally brought into legal existence represent only the carefully selected residum of numerous projects and principles, which, in the meantime, have been sedulously tested and silently eliminated in Committee.

"I believe that the great difficulties with which the Committee have had to deal in framing the present Bill, have arisen out of the exceeding complexity of the relations of the population of Oudh,—on the one hand to the soil, and on the other hand to the State. That population is composed, broadly speaking, of three dissimilar and yet closely inter-related classes. In the first place, there are the taluqdars; then there are the rest of the proprietors and the village communities; and lastly, there are other under-proprietors and subordinate holders. The taluqdars are directly responsible to Government for the payment of the land-revenue assessed on their estates; as are also the other proprietors and the village communities; while the under-proprietors and subordinate holders pay the revenue assessed on their lands to a taluqdar or some other superior proprietor in addition to the share of the profits to which he is entitled. The Government of India, therefore, in legislating on the subject of land-revenue in Oudh, has had to consider most carefully, not only the relative rights of the taluqdars, superior proprietors, under-proprietors, and subordinate holders, but also the grounds on which those rights repose in ancient usage and custom, as well as the conditions whereby they should be regulated and defined in accordance with modern requirements. In fact, the task which the Government has had to undertake, has been to reconcile, as far as possible, the vested rights and interests of the taluqdars with the interests of subordinate holders, the interests of the cultivator, the interests of the State, and the interests of the soil itself. Now I should certainly have thought that a Legislature, thus practically engaged in the conscientious endeavours to work out to a just solution one of the most perplexing—though at the same time one of the most interesting—problems in legislation, might have fairly and reasonably reckoned on receiving from a publicist so eminent as M. de Laveleye, should he deign to notice their labours well, if not a sympathetic interest in the difficulty of those labours, at least a perfectly impartial recognition of their results. But I will now ask the Hon'ble Members to allow me to read to them a few passages from the work by M. de Laveleye, to which I have referred; and if those passages are not already in the recollection of the Hon'ble Members, I am sure they will hear them with considerable surprise:

"'In Oudh,' says M. Laveleye, 'the British Government has considered the taluqdars as the sole proprietors of the soil, *without any reserve whatever on behalf of the interests of the subordinate holders.*' M. de Laveleye then adds, that although Government instituted an enquiry into the question, whether the ryots possessed any rights at all in connection with the soil they cultivated, yet they (*ryots*) were *terrified* into answering that enquiry with a negative. And then, after having drawn this double indictment against the British Government for bribery and intimidation (bribery in our dealings with the taluqdars—intimidation in our dealings with the ryots), M. de Laveleye continues:—'In Oudh the State (*i.e.*, the British Government) *has stipulated no guarantee whatever for the ryot.*' This is a fault and something more. It is a crime—the crime of high treason against humanity. Well now, what can one say of assertions like this, unless it be what Horace Walpole, I believe, said of a certain lady of his acquaintance: 'She has,' he said, 'as good a set of teeth as any woman can have, who has only three teeth, and each of them black.' Is it too much to say of such a passage as this, that it is as full, candid, accurate as any passage can be which contains only three statements and each of them false? M. de Laveleye is, I believe, a member of the Cobden Club; and if so, he is certainly one of the most distinguished members of it, and I have no doubt whatever that to his numerous continental readers this circumstance will have been an all-sufficient guarantee for the accuracy of his statements upon the subjects of Indian Legislation. But what are the facts? Now, I speak here in the presence of experienced Indian legislators. There is not a single hon'ble member sitting at this table who will not be able to correct me immediately, if I am unwarranted in asserting, that in the whole history of the land legislation for Oudh, there has been no period at which the Legislature of this empire has ignored the existence of proprietary rights in the soil of that province other than those of the taluqdars; that at no period has it disregarded the interests of the subordinate holders of those rights; that at no period has it omitted to take elaborate precautions for the protection of the tenant and the ryot from any abuse of powers, which, though recognized by our generosity, have always been restrained by our justice. I appeal to the record of our land legislation in Oudh, which I now hold in my hand. Act XXVI of 1866 is exclusively devoted to the affirmation and definition of the claims of the subordinate proprietors in Oudh.

"Now, this Act was passed within ten years after the Annexation of Oudh; but its very preamble attests the pre-existence of rules and regulations issued by the Government of India for—what are the words?—'the better determination of claims by persons possessed of subordinate rights of property in Oudh.' Again I turn to Act XIX of 1868, and I find the Act to be one elaborate Code of law for the maintenance of subordinate proprietary rights, and for the protection of tenants in Oudh. Section 5 of this Act defines the rights of occupancy, which include those of the ryots. Sections 22—26 secure to the tenants of Oudh the right of compensation for improvements; Chapter IV limits the maximum rates of rent; Chapter V strictly circumscribes the power of ejectments, and the same consistent tendency of our land legislation for Oudh is continued in this direction, and carried on by the Bill we hope to pass to-day. Section 25 of that Bill, subject to important exemptions, gives the right to resume rent-free grants; and again section 135 secures to the State comprehensive powers for the rescue and preservation of the interests of tenants whose land is sold for arrears of revenue.

"Now, I make no apology to Hon'ble Members for having inflicted upon their patience this reference to facts, with which they are all thoroughly familiar, because I am sure they will feel that on an occasion like the present, and as the executive head of the Government of India, I need make to the Members of this Legislature no excuse for endeavouring to refute the unfounded aspersions cast upon their policy by so distinguished a critic of it as M. de Laveleye. And, indeed, if some echo of my words should reach beyond this room, I trust it may tend to confirm the taluqdars of Oudh in that consideration and recognition, which I am bound to say they have given to the many and great difficulties involved in the task undertaken by this Government, and also to the impartial and conscientious spirit in which the Government has endeavoured to perform that task in legislating upon a subject, which materially concerns the interests of other classes in Oudh besides their own."

CHAPTER VII.

ENHANCEMENT OF RENT.

His Honor the Lieutenant-Governor (Sir George Couper), addressing the Taluqdars of Oudh at the Agricultural Exhibition of 1881, said :—

"You will have heard that it is proposed to pass a new law in Bengal, the effect of which will be to raise almost every cultivator in that province to the rank of an occupancy tenant. This has been found necessary, because it is the opinion of officers serving in Bengal, that the tenantry there have been unduly harassed and grievously oppressed by the exactions of the landlords. Now I have been among you, and been your friend and well-wisher for the last quarter of a century, and I do not think I should be acting the part of a true friend and well-wisher were I to conceal the fact, indeed if I were not to tell you plainly that the same thing has often been said of you, although it may be by people who have not had that knowledge and experience of the circumstances of the province which would entitle their opinions to be received with respect. For I would fain hope and believe that you, who may be said to have been for centuries the leaders of your people, do feel a kindly sympathy for them, and do take a warm personal interest in their well-being; and these are sentiments which can hardly be expected from men who have recently acquired their estates by purchase, and who regard them as a mere commercial speculation, their sole business with which is to wring from the wretched villagers the last fraction of a rupee. Still you cannot be unaware how dangerous it is not to have the means of answering an accusation, however untrue and unjust that accusation in itself may be."

The charge which has been brought against the taluqdars by men who are totally ignorant of the true condition of the province, and of the relations existing between the landlords and their tenants, can be refuted, as His Honor justly says, by a reference to accurate rent-rolls and trustworthy village records. It is certainly from these papers alone that the true condition of the peasantry can be clearly ascertained; and we would refer those who accuse the taluqdars of rack-renting their ryots to the rent-rolls which every landholder keeps in his record-room. A strict examination of these papers will show to all unprejudiced persons that the charge is utterly unfounded. It is obvious that all landlords must keep "accurate rent-rolls" in their offices, as without this it is utterly impossible to collect rents and to manage an estate. Any person who really desires to know the true circumstances and condition of the peasantry of Oudh may any day satisfy himself by an examination of the rent-rolls that the taluqdars, instead of harassing and oppressing their tenants by undue exactions, take a most tender care of their interests, which are bound up with their own.

Let us see now how far these charges are borne out by official records.

The following table will give us the provincial average rent per acre for land suited for wheat, the great spring crop of Oudh, from 1872 to 1880 :—

			Rs.	As.	P.
1872	...	...	6	9	2⅓
1873	...	...	6	12	6
1874	...	...	6	12	0⅓
1875	...	...	6	6	8½
1876	...	...	5	13	0
1877	...	...	6	5	11½
1878	...	...	6	8	2
1879	...	...	6	8	2
1880	...	...	6	7	2

We would ask an impartial reader whether there is any trace of rack-renting in the table given above. Does it not clearly show that the average rent for the nine years under review has been pretty much the same? The slight difference of a few annas per acre is explained by the character of the seasons, and the average produce of land per acre in each year. In one year, 1876, the average rent was actually less than the normal average, and this fact plainly shows that the taluqdars would rather suffer themselves than harass their tenants in any way. It should be remembered that the settlement of most of the estates was completed during these nine years, and the majority of the estates were most heavily assessed. Speaking of the revenue balances in 1873, and of the embarrassed condition of the land-owning classes, which is denoted by their existence, the Chief Commissioner says :—

"To bad seasons, disastrous as had been their effects, could not alone be ascribed the state of affairs, and reference was made to other probable causes which would require attentive consideration. The most important question with which the Administration was concerned, was the extent to which the people had been affected by the operations of the settlement, and the pressure, in certain districts, of the revised assessments recently imposed."

Apart from cases of real over-assessment, there is no doubt that the action of the Settlement Department (we read in the Revenue Report for 1873) did, in many instances, press heavily on the people. In some districts, notably Fyzabad, Gonda, Kheri, and parts of Sultanpore, at a time of supposed financial pressure, the revision of the assessment was hurried on, and a greatly enhanced demand was imposed before the Settlement Officer had had time to adjust the rights and liabilities of the various sharers and under-proprietors affected by this operation. It is not difficult to understand that a course such as this necessarily entails great hardship on the persons directly responsible for the Government revenue. It becomes extremely difficult for them to meet the whole of the Government demand, and they are not in a position to recover from their co-sharers and subordinate holders their fair quota of the increase. And the distress which must result from the sudden imposition of a largely enhanced demand, does not require demonstration. What with the too early introduction of the revised assessment, the excessive immediate enhancement of the Government demand,

and the calamities of the season, the land-owning classes in Oudh have been in a very deplorable condition for successive years. But with all this can anybody point to a single authenticate instance of rack-renting? The table we have given above proves beyond the shadow of a doubt that anything like rack-renting is utterly unknown in Oudh. There has been of course a very slight variation in the rates, but it will be found, on examination, that it is no more than what the capacity of the soil can bear. A landlord on whose estate the Government demand has been raised at the regular settlement would naturally seek to increase his rent-roll; but it will be seen from the table given above that there has been no sudden enhancement of the landlord's demand. The landlord, more considerate than inexperienced Settlement Officers, increased the rent whenever such an increase was found to be fair, with care and deliberation, weighing every circumstance in favour and against his tenant. The sudden enhanced demand pressed heavily upon him, and he would rather go to the money-lender, and involve himself in debt to meet the Government demand, than harass his poor tenants. Whenever, as we said, an increase of rent has been found absolutely necessary, the increase was made gradually after fully ascertaining the circumstances under which an increased rent was put on. Increase of rent there must be when there has been a general increase of the produce of land, and a consequent enhancement of the Government demand. The Government assessment is enhanced on the ostensible ground that there has been an increased produce of the land assessed. It is the object of the Settlement Officers to make the assessment everywhere bear a fair proportion to the capacity of the soil, and where the assessment is enhanced on this ground, it is reasonable to expect that the landlord also, who has to meet the Government demand, would try to raise his rent in such a manner that it may also bear a fair proportion to the capacities of the soil. The moment, however, a landlord wishes to raise his demand, a general cry is made by pseudo-philanthropists of rack-renting, and harassing and oppressing the ryots by undue exactions. This is certainly not fair. If you expect the landlord to be generous, the

Government must first of all be generous to them. Now that the settlement has been completed, the equitable proportion between Government revenue and the landlord's demand is being gradually fixed. The variation, slight though it be, which we observe in the table, clearly indicates that an equalization has very nearly been arrived at, and that no possible ground for complaint exists at the present moment. The thirty years' settlement, however, will soon be over, and before the province has had time to recover from the harassing action of the Settlement Department, the evil effects of these constantly-recurring settlements will be experienced again. So long as Oudh is not blessed with a Permanent Settlement, there is no security against over-assessment in one form or another, and the taluqdars will be continually subject to those charges which "the changing prejudice of the hour may bring against them."

CHAPTER VIII.

NOTICES OF EJECTMENT.

It has been said that in Oudh "hundreds of thousands of cultivators are always liable to ejectment for no better cause than the *will* of the landlord." It is of importance to see how far this charge is just.

This charge refers to the notices of ejectment which, under the Oudh Rent Act, are issued by landlords against tenants.

Prior to the passing of the Oudh Rent Act it was customary in Oudh for landlords, who wished to raise the rent of a tenant, to serve him with a notice of enhancement through the Courts; but no such notices being recognized in the Act, a practice has sprung up of serving a tenant with a notice of ejectment when the real object is simply to raise his rent. The process is this: a tenant refuses to engage to pay an enhanced rent and he receives a notice of ejectment, and if this notice is not *successfully* contested in the Courts his tenancy ceases, and he must either quit the lands or come to terms with his landlord. (Administration Report, 1872-73, p. 60.)

"The fact is," writes the Chief Commissioner in 1871, "that, owing to the pressure put upon us to bring the settlement to a close, the enhanced rates of assessment are declared before the rights of the underholders have been judicially determined." It is obviously not right that the whole burden of the increased demand should fall upon the landlord; and he consequently looks to his tenants for an enhancement of their rents. Naturally they are reluctant to enter into his views without a certain degree of pressure, and the only mode he has of coercing them is by a suit for ejectment under the Rent Act. Such a suit is in short a mere notice to the tenant that his rent will be enhanced, although it bears the ugly name of ejectment. (Administration Report, 1870-71, p. 25.)

It will be seen then that the Oudh Rent Act has prescribed a procedure, in form somewhat cumbrous—but so far favorable to the tenant—for the ejectment of tenants, or the enhancement of the rents of tenants, who refuse to agree to the terms of the landlord. In either case a notice of ejectment is to be served on the tenant through the tehsildar of his tehsil. It is very well known that in a large majority of cases the real object of the landlord in the issue of notices is to get rid of habitual defaulters, to recover the arrears of rent, or to share in the proceeds of the high prices that may be ruling for the time, and procure an increase to his rental. The Rent Act contains no provision enabling a landlord to apply to the Courts to fix a fair rent on his tenants-at-will who may be holding at low rates; the only means he at present has of forcing such tenants to agree to an enhancement is to serve these notices of ejectment on them. In 99 cases out of a 100 the landlord has no desire to eject the tenant from his holding; his only object in issuing the notice is to get what he considers a full rent for the land occupied by the tenant. Even at settlement time, when the revenue payable by a proprietor was largely enhanced in consequence of the revised assessment being based on the rental his estate would yield were the rates prevailing in the neighbourhood enforced, the landlord could get no assistance, either from the Settlement or the District Courts, in enforcing these rents; and if he could not get his tenants to agree to them, he was obliged, to protect himself, to issue these notices of ejectment.

The statistics now available establish the fact that the main incentives to a landlord, in issuing these notices, are either a wish to get rid of a worthless tenant, or a desire to compel a tenant to agree to an enhancement of rent. So far as can be ascertained, the landlords are influenced at least as often by the first as by the second of these motives, but the enhancement of the rent is very frequently their object. In attaining this end, however, they meet with but partial success, and at best the procedure is cumbrous and round about.

"The Commissioner of the Fyzabad Division," we read in the Revenue Report for 1875, "before whom a large number of these cases have in successive years passed in appeal, says that he can comparatively seldom trace enmity as the reason for the issue of the notice, whereas he frequently finds that the person evicted is a well-to-do, high caste man, who has managed to secure some of the best lands in a village, and by one pretence or another has contrived to avoid payment of even the proper corn-rent for which he has agreed. Other officers bear similar testimony to a general absence of malice, and Sir George Couper nowhere finds any reason to alter his opinion that landlords very rarely abuse the power of ejectment." Nay, the testimony is general to the absence of any vindictive feeling, or abuse by the landlords of the powers they possess under the Rent Act. (Revenue Report, 1877.)

A careful and laborious enquiry into the result of the issue of notices of ejectment was made in 1872-73. The result of this close enquiry was considered to be very satisfactory. The steady decrease in the number of these notices, taking all the drawbacks of season into consideration, tended to show that the relations of the landlord and tenant were on a very satisfactory footing. As a means of raising the rents, these notices, in the majority of instances, failed, and it was fully proved that the demand for cultivators was sufficiently great to render it most impolitic in a landlord to use his power of ejectment in the case of an industrious tenant who pays a fair rent. Nor did it appear that, as a general rule, this was done. The attempt to obtain a reduction of rent by means of a threat on the part of a tenant to relinquish his holding was, so far as could be determined, more successful than the landlord's measures to enhance; and the tenants appear to be well aware of their opportunities.

After giving the subject the very best consideration, the Chief Commissioner was of opinion that cases in which a good tenant is altogether evicted is very rare; and that, as a rule, this action is taken against bad tenants only. In support of this position, it may be mentioned that upwards of 59 per cent. of the evicted tenants are Brahmins and Thakurs, who are notoriously the worst cultivators, and the most recalcitrant rent-payers in the province. "If the truth of this position," says the Chief Commissioner, "be conceded, it is difficult to understand how we can blame the landlords, or to what other action we can suggest they should have recourse. It is the same all the world over; and Sir George Couper opines, that in England a tenant-at-will who will neither cultivate his land properly nor pay his rent promptly would be very speedily got rid of; and, if either of these facts were established, the landlord would not be held blameworthy."

It will be noticed that there is a correlative to this account. Just as the landlord disliking his tenant, or desirous of a higher rent, reaches his end by a notice of ejectment, so the tenant, dissatisfied with his landlord or rent, reaches his end by a notice of relinquishment. As, in the one case, the landlord seeks to get rid of a bad tenant who will not pay his rent, or desires to induce the tenant to agree to an enhancement; so, in the other case, the tenant who gives in a notice of relinquishment, has, in most instances, no desire to throw up his holding, but either seeks to obtain a reduction of his rent, or meets the landlord's demand for a higher rent by a threat to vacate the land. With regard to the notices of ejectment, the bulk of the tenants proceeded against are of the higher castes, who are ordinarily the worst cultivators and the worst rent-payers. Though Brahmins and Rajpoots constitute but a sixth of the population, upwards of half of the notices of ejectment are directed against these men; while the case is reversed in regard to relinquishments, the lower castes contributing upwards of 70 per cent. It is almost invariably the case that an increase in the profits of agriculturists causes a rise in the number of notices of ejectment and a fall in the number of those of relinquishment, whilst the results of a less favorable season are the reverse. This is a result naturally to be expected in a season during which the demand for grain for export causes high prices to prevail, and favorably affects the position of the cultivator. This will account for the fact of there being 38,636 notices of ejectment in 1877, while in 1873 the number was 16,476 only. We read in the Revenue Report for 1873—"In the last Revenue

Administration Report it was said that the autumn harvest of the agricultural year 1280 *Fasli* had been above the average, and sufficiently plenteous to give the people heart to recover from the grievous disasters which had, in previous seasons, befallen them. There was then evey reason to hope that the spring crop would have yielded a full return, and thus further contribute to improve the condition of the agricultural classes. But these fair hopes were not realized; for, by the failure of the usual winter rain, much of the rabi was withered and destroyed, and the outturn was, generally, lighter than usual. The Lucknow and Unao Districts suffered from a special visitation in the shape of a severe hailstorm, which occurred on the 7th March, when the crops were fast ripening, and most liable to injury from the falling hail." The year 1877 was more prosperous, and although there was a failure of the rains at the end of the year, the harvest was more plenteous. With a more prosperous season an increase in the number of notices of ejectment was to be expected. Land was in greater demand with cultivators, and landlords were, therefore, in a position to demand enhanced rents and get rid of their worst tenants.

The number of notices of ejectment issued in 1877 are classified as follows, according to the reasons given for their issue :—

On account of tenants' default, 21,805, or 55 per cent.

On account of tenants' inability to cultivate, 1,956, or 5 per cent.

In order to enhance rent, 10,134, or 26 per cent.

Other causes, 5,242, or 14 per cent.

We find in the official return that the number of holdings in the hands of tenants-at-will, in 1877, was 1,394,607. Now no one can find fault with a landlord for issuing notices of ejectmet on account of their tenants' habitual default and inability to cultivate. The tenants on whom these notices were served are those who either would not, or could not, pay the rent. They harass the landlord, and to protect himself the landlord is obliged to issue these notices. An understanding is soon arrived at—the tenant pays his rent, and cultivates his holding as usual. Leaving out the notices which were issued for these reasons, we have still to account for 15,376 notices. The words "*other causes*" is vague and misleading, and may imply anything. But let that pass.

We have shown above that notices of enhancement were issued because the landlords naturally wished in 1877, which was a comparatively prosperous year and high prices prevailed, to share in the profits. The number of notices for enhancement, which were issued during the year, does not imply that the tenants were evicted. Far from it. In 999 cases out of a 1,000, tenants, as a rule, accept the enhanced rent and retain their holdings. The notices under the miscellaneous head, when properly investigated, would disclose the fact that the majority of the tenants on whom they were served, without deserting the villages in which they live, are cultivating land in other villages; and that a number of them have adopted some other trade. Of those who actually abandon agriculture, a considerable number pursued it only in addition to some more regular and permanent calling; for, though the majority of those who are classed as having taken to other callings became day-labourers, there are to be found, if the details given in the official returns be closely examined, a large number of shop-keepers, traders, contractors, and even bankers.

A case of real eviction is extremely rare. The investigation showed in 1873, which was a disastrous year, that "there had been only about one real eviction of a tenant in every 20 villages." (Revenue Report, 1873.)

The Deputy Commissioner of Gonda, speaking of the large number of these notices in Bishambarpur estate, which is under Government management, says (Revenue Report, 1873, p. 53):—"Many tenants, especially of the Brahmin and Chatri castes, struck for lower rents, which, as Superintendent of the Court of Wards, and on due consideration of their circumstances, I saw no sufficient reason to allow: while several refused to take *pattas* on any terms. Notices were, therefore, issued to all such recusant cultivators, which, however, resulted in ultimate eviction to very few. The circumstances of the year were such as to demand firmness on the part of landlords, while at the same time they had due regard to the difficulties of their tenants;

otherwise, estates would have run down with a rapidity which it would have taken years to recover from."

Comments on the above are superfluous. This Report of the Deputy Commissioner of Gonda is of exceptional interest, and correctly explains the action of the landlord in the majority of the notices issued. In 1879, one of the Deputy Commissioners considered that the compilation of the *khusras* had enlightened landlords and tenants as to the real area of the latter's holdings, and landlords were, for the first time, able to ascertain exactly what lands were held by *sirholders* and other *hakdars* in excess of the lands decreed to them, and that this explains, in most cases, the increase in the notices of ejectment, a comparatively large number having been issued to bring tenants to terms for the land occupied by them in excess of their decreed holdings. There can be no doubt, says His Honor the Lieutenant-Governor, that "Deputy Commissioners are right in ascribing them in part to the more accurate knowledge of the extent, nature, and rent of the various holdings afforded by improved village papers." The Deputy Commissioner of Lucknow, whose opinion is of great value, justly says that (in 1879) "the number of notices issued is no real index to the number of tenants evicted, as it is a fact that the majority accepted the higher rent demanded, and cultivated the land for which notices of ejectment were issued."

Sir George Couper, who closely watched the operation of the Rent Act for a large number of years, thus writes on this vexed question: "The results are generally confirmations of the opinions which have, from time to time, been expressed by the Lieutenant-Governor. Landlords resort to the power of ejectment mainly to get rid of worthless tenants (a perfectly legitimate ground of action), or to compel a tenant to agree to an enhancement of rent, or to pay rent for land previously held rent-free. So far as has been ascertained, the landlords do very seldom abuse their powers in order to obtain an enhancement. In many cases, no doubt, the landlord merely seeks to get a reasonable rent for the occupation of his land, and it is an unfortunate feature of the existing law, and one which His Honor has unsuccessfully endeavoured to have remedied, that the only way in which a landlord can encompass this entirely justifiable object, if the tenant will not listen to reason, is to incur the odium of serving a notice of ejectment.*

I have come to the conclusion of my subject. Much might be written on the advantages of the Taluqdari system, but I advisedly refrain from adding more, and prefer to leave the facts and arguments which I have brought forward in this work to speak for themselves. How the taluqdars have endeavoured to discharge the trust reposed in them, the history of the last twenty-four years abundantly shows. To those however who calumniate the taluqdars without just cause, I would recall the noble words of the greatest of modern poets:—

> "Good name, in man or woman, dear my lord,
> Is the immediate jewel of their souls.
> Who steals my purse, steals trash; 't is something, nothing;
> 'T was mine, 't is his, and has been slave to thousands;
> But he that filches from me my good name,
> Robs me of that which not enriches him,
> And makes me poor indeed."

---

* The varieties of tenures in Oudh deserve notice. The land of Oudh is held amongst the various classes of landlords in the porportions shown in the following table:—

			Acres.		
Taluqdars	...	...	8,797,560	60	per cent.
Zemindars	...	...	976,803	6	"
Village communities	...	...	4,396,078	30	"
Revenue-free	...	...	361,928	2	"
Waste-land grants	...	...	213,297	1	"

Among the taluqdars, while there are several with magnificent incomes, the great majority of them are possessed of estates paying on the average a revenue of Rs. 17,000, or Rs. 18,000. The zemindari holding are on a much smaller scale, with an average revenue of Rs. 300 to 400; those of the communities are larger in area, but so subdivided among the coparceners that the average of the proprietary profits is represented in the returns to be under Rs. 43 a year to the shareholders, or less than Rs. 4 a month. The coparceners add to their means by the wages of service, &c., but the statistics show an amount of subdivision which leaves but little advantage to the individual sharers.

Of the cultivated area of the Province, 8,276,174 acres, the agricultural occupancy is in the hands of the following classes:—

Sub-proprietary *Sir*	...	...	190,604	acres.
Birtdars and others	...	...	234,338	"
Tenants in occupancy right	...	...	103,720	"
Tenants-at-will	...	...	638,596	"
Rent-free holders	...	...	193,491	"
Proprietary *Sir* (about)	...	...	1,164,425	"